Phillips Brooks

The spiritual Man and other Sermons

Phillips Brooks
The spiritual Man and other Sermons
ISBN/EAN: 9783743349346
Manufactured in Europe, USA, Canada, Australia, Japa
Cover: Foto ©Lupo / pixelio.de

Manufactured and distributed by brebook publishing software (www.brebook.com)

Phillips Brooks

The spiritual Man and other Sermons

THE SPIRITUAL MAN
AND OTHER SERMONS

BY THE SAME AUTHOR.

SERMONS PREACHED IN TRINITY CHURCH, BOSTON, IN 1879.

Crown 8vo, cloth, 4s. 6d.

THE LIGHT OF THE WORLD AND OTHER SERMONS.

Crown 8vo, cloth, 3s. 6d.

THE SPIRITUAL MAN

AND OTHER SERMONS

BY

PHILLIPS BROOKS
RECTOR OF TRINITY CHURCH, BOSTON

LONDON
R. D. DICKINSON, 89 FARRINGDON STREET
1891

CONTENTS.

Sermon I.
THE SPIRITUAL MAN.

PAGE

"Behold, thou shalt call a nation that thou knowest not, and nations which know not thee shall run unto thee, because of the Lord thy God and the Holy One of Israel, for He hath glorified thee" (Isaiah lv. 5), . 1

Sermon II.
THE UNBROKEN CHAIN.

"But I would not have you to be ignorant, brethren, concerning them which are asleep, that ye sorrow not, even as others which have no hope. For if we believe that Jesus died and rose again, even so them also which sleep in Jesus will God bring with Him" (1 Thess. iv. 13, 14), ... 20

Sermon III.
THE MAGDALENE.

"And, behold, a woman in the city, which was a sinner" (St. Luke vii. 37), ... 34

Sermon IV.
THE TEMPTATION OF CHRIST.

"The temptation" (Matt. iv. 3, 4), ... 47

SERMON V.

THE FEEDING OF THE MULTITUDE.

"When Jesus then lifted up His eyes and saw a great company come unto Him, He saith unto Philip: Whence shall we buy bread, that these may eat?" (St. John vi. 5), ... 59

SERMON VI.

LESSONS FROM THE LIFE OF JESUS.

"Unto you is born this day, in the city of David, a Saviour" (St. Luke ii. 10), ... 74

SERMON VII.

THE TRUE TEST.

"Forbid him not" (St Luke ix. 49, 50), ... 88

SERMON VIII.

JUDGMENTS OF LIFE.

Psalm x., ... 102

SERMON IX.

NOT BEING MIXED WITH FAITH.

Heb. iv. 2, ... 109

SERMON X.

LIBERTY OF THE CHRISTIAN LIFE.

"If the Son, therefore, shall make you free, ye shall be free indeed" (St. John viii. 36), ... 127

SERMON XI.

IMMORTALITY.

"In that He died, He died unto sin once; but in that He liveth, He liveth unto God" (Romans vi. 13), . . 141

CONTENTS.

SERMON XII.
THE ETERNAL LIFE.

"And this is life eternal:.that they might know Thee, the only true God, and Jesus Christ, Whom Thou hast sent" (St. John xvii. 3), ... **155**

SERMON XIII.
THE RESCUE OF A SOUL.

"And He said: A certain man had two sons" (St. Luke xv. 11), ... **174**

SERMON XIV.
"LIKE AS A FATHER."

Psalm ciii. 13, ... **184**

SERMON XV.
CRYING AFTER CHRIST.

"The Canaanitish woman" (Matt. xv. 21-28), . . . **203**

SERMON XVI.
THE REWARDS OF VICTORY.

"He that overcometh shall inherit all things" (Rev. xxi. 7), **217**

SERMON XVII.
ST. PAUL AT PHILIPPI.

"Therefore, my brethren dearly beloved and longed for, my joy and crown, so stand fast in the Lord, my dearly beloved" (Phil. iv. 1), ... **236**

SERMON XVIII.
THE EPISTLE TO THE COLOSSIANS.

"Paul, an apostle of Jesus Christ by the will of God, and Timotheus, our brother, to the saints and faithful brethren in Christ which are at Colosse" (Col. i. 1, 2), ... **247**

Sermon XIX.

TWO EPISTLES.

"Unto Timothy, my own son in the faith: Grace, mercy, and peace, from God our Father and Jesus Christ our Lord" (1 Tim. i. 2). "For I am now ready to be offered, and the time of my departure is at hand" (2 Tim. iv. 6), ... 258

Sermon XX.

EXPOSITION OF THE NINETEENTH PSALM.

"The heavens declare the glory of God," etc. (Psalm xix.), 272

Sermon XXI.

EXPOSITION OF THE TWENTY-THIRD PSALM.

Psalm xxiii., ... 281

Sermon XXII.

EXPOSITION OF THE FIFTY-NINTH PSALM.

Psalm lix., ... 290

Sermon XXIII.

TRUE GREATNESS.

"Thy gentleness hath made me great" (Psalm xviii. 35), 301

Sermon XXIV.

MAKING ALL THINGS NEW.

Making all things new, ... 304

Sermon XXV.

THE GREAT DEEDS OF CHRIST.

The great deeds of Christ, ... 308

THE SPIRITUAL MAN.

"*Behold, thou shalt call a nation that thou knowest not, and nations which know not thee shall run unto thee, because of the Lord thy God and the Holy One of Israel; for He hath glorified thee.*"
—ISAIAH lv. 5.

ISAIAH, the poet of prophets, was the great patriot of the Jews. Every truest and best patriot must have something of the poet and prophet in him. He must be something of a poet, because he must look below the surface of his country's prosperity or disaster, and see wherein the real soul of her blessings and her sorrows lies. He must be something of a prophet that he may take in all his country's long life, and not be misled by too narrow a study of her present condition. Such a patriot was Christ. He could not be deluded by enormous stores and stately structures so long as the heart of Jerusalem was selfish and corrupt. He could not be satisfied with the peace and quiet of the moment while His ears heard afar off the thunder of the coming storm. It was the poet and the prophet in His soul that loved His city, and so He could upbraid her as no other of her children could. And He could look abroad, and tell in saddened tones how from the east and west and north and south the citizens of other lands would come and take the places of which His own beloved city had proved herself unworthy.

We need far more than we possess of the lofty patriotism of Isaiah and of Jesus. Plenty of pride in our city and our nation, plenty of boasting there is about their wealth and greatness; but of that fullest patriotism which corresponds to the fullest friendship we have far too little. That fullest patriotism is on one side the extension of the personal life, keeping its vigour and distinctness, and on the other side it is the specialising of the enthusiasm of humanity, keeping its largeness and inspiration. May it not truly be said that he who would be a patriot with such a patriotism as that must be both poet and prophet, like Isaiah or like Christ?

It would seem as if Judea must have been a country peculiarly adapted to call out the best kind of spiritual patriotism. Her children firmly believed that she was consecrated to the highest purposes of God. She was full of the idea of spirituality. She lay there between her mighty neighbours, with Assyria on one side of her and Egypt on the other, and while they represented wealth and power she distinctly stood for spirituality and holiness. Very interesting always is this representative character of nations. The nations stand in history each with its nature shining in its face—Greece with its passion for knowledge, Rome with its organised and compacted strength, and all the modern nations making each its distinct and recognisable contribution to the great family of nations, the members of which are not monotonously uniform, but embody the most interesting kind of unity in their great diversity of character. In the midst of this beautiful variety stands the nation of the Jews, for ever representing spiritual life.

Sometimes there come to us wonderings and questionings when we look at this variety of national character, each nation offering some type of life or some moral quality peculiarly its own—wonderings and questionings which correspond to those with which we ponder on the variety of individual characters which make up the united society in the midst of which we live. A new nation is born like a new man. A nation such as ours comes forth, latest and best equipped, into the light of day. What shall we expect of this last born of time? Shall we stand by and watch to see what special quality is to be embodied here—whether a new nation of learning, or a new nation of power, or a new nation of wealth, or a new nation of philosophy and religion is going to occupy this continent so long reserved for some one of the last experiments of human life? Does there not sometimes come to us another dream, which is that somehow on this vast latest field the types which elsewhere history has developed may find some kind of union; that here may come a larger national character capable of comprehending all; that here may come wealth, not base, selfish, and vulgar, as wealth is when it lives alone, but pervaded and sanctified by spiritual ambitions and the consciousness of holy uses; that here may come religion, not only as the personal delight and education of the single soul, but also as the organised salvation of humanity; that here Law may learn the lesson of Grace and become not merely the restraint but the development of crude and sinful men; that learning here may prove itself a truly moral force and make men better as it makes them wise? Can any thoughtful man look into the future of our country and not dream some such great dream as this? There is something better which must come some day than merely another and another of these partial, one-sided studies of humanity, devoted to the development of some single quality or type of life. Sometime the universal nation, like the universal man, must come, in which quality shall blend with quality, each lending the other at once its richness and its restraint, and so the complete nationality, the true kingdom of God, shall be established.

Let us indulge that dream; but meanwhile let us rejoice that every nation stands for something, that God has ordained that in each national life some excellence of human nature shall be embodied. When we feel this, then we can enter into the joy of Isaiah, his triumph in the thought that, because that which his nation stood for was the noblest and most precious thing of all, therefore all other nations, however much greater they might be in the wealth of their treasuries and in the number of their armies, must own the superior power of his Jerusalem and be drawn by its attractions. This is the idea which is in the words that he hears God speaking in the text, "*Behold, thou shalt call a nation that thou knowest not, and nations which know not thee shall run unto thee, because of the Lord thy God*". We cannot tell just what picture was in Isaiah's mind and hovering before his eyes. We do not know just what degree of visible sovereignty he hoped to see Jerusalem attain—but the essential idea is clear enough. He believed that all people were to turn to the Hebrews because the Hebrews were especially God's people, because the nations would all feel that the God whom they all must have had been made known with the completest clearness and purity among the Jews. How clearly that prophecy has been fulfilled all subsequent history can tell. The Hebrew Book, the Hebrew men, have been the magnets which have drawn the world's devotion. Into the midst of Judaism was set the Incarnation of the Godhead, which, shining out from thence, has been the light which has enlightened every man. The Bible is the very epitome of Judaism, and the Bible is the centre more and more completely of the world's devotion.

"*Nations that know not thee shall run unto thee.*" What words like those could prophesy the scenes which have come in these modern days,—Englishmen, Italians, Germans, Americans seeking the law of inspiration of their life in the old Hebrew Bible, turning those venerable pages to learn how they ought to live, drinking at the fountain of the ideas of Israel the strength and cleansing which their own modern life demanded. We abase the Jew, sometimes we sneer at him and despise him—but we live upon the thoughts which he has thought, and the visions which he saw of God make the very sunshine of our life.

I think that we do not take in as we should this picture of the Hebrew standing as the great Image of Spirituality in the world's life, and of the power which he has exercised thereby. But it is not of that that I mainly wish to speak to-day. I am thinking of it as a sort of parable. It represents to me the way in which the *spiritual* man everywhere is meant to be the central man, the fire, the inspiration, the illumination and attraction of mankind. There is a certain sort of man who is among his fellow-men what Israel was among the nations. Other men are richer, other men are mightier, than he. Often their riches and their might seem to crowd upon him, as Assyria and Egypt crowded upon Judea, and leave him no chance to breathe; but in the long run he is the King of life. Men turn to him in their deepest moments and with their deepest needs. He helps men very different from, very much greater than, himself. To become such a man is the truest and worthiest ambition of a human soul. To be content to live without being such a man in some degree shows a pusillanimous and feeble nature.

Let us not seem to be claiming preposterous honour for any one kind of man, until first we have examined what sort of man he is. This Jew man among his brethren, this man of spirituality—what is it to be *spiritual?* Ah! that old question! How men have asked it of themselves or one another! What answers they have given to it! How they have tried to make themselves think that they were spiritual when really they were only formal or only sentimental! How men have given up the question in despair! How they have said, "It is impossible for me. That man, that woman, may be spiritual, but not I!" Is there, then, any answer? Can we tell what it is to be a *spiritual* man and to live *spiritually?* I think we can, certainly. *A spiritual man is a man who deals with the spirits and the souls of things, and lives for them.* Is that intelligible? Here are two generous men. Both of them give their money freely. One of them is spiritually generous, the other is unspiritually generous. What is the difference? One of them loves generosity for itself, the other loves it only for the result it brings. One of them rejoices in the very fact of sharing with his brethren that which God has given him. The other wants certain things done—the hospital built, the poor man fed—and, since giving money is the way to get that done, he gives the money. Do you see the difference?

Here are two money-making men. One of them values his money for the comfortable uses he can put it to; the other is not satisfied until he has got at the heart of riches, and absorbed his wealth into his character, and made himself by it a richer nature and a fuller man. Here are two religious men. One of them rejoices in religion for the good it does. He says that it secures order in this world, and saves suffering in the world to come. Another man feeds his heart on the very substance of religion itself. To commune with God, and love Him and obey Him, is the very life of life. Life would be death without it. Here are two scholars. One of them studies for the advantages that learning brings; the other studies for the pure joy of knowing. Truth and the human mind meet and satisfy each other. You see that everywhere there is the spiritual and the unspiritual way of doing and being everything. Spirituality is not an attainment, an acquisition of the nature; it is a quality of the nature. It is not a thing to be; it is a way of being everything.

It is easy to extend such a distinction from special employments to the whole character and conduct of a life. Two men live. And to one of them life means the doing of certain works, the passing through certain experiences. To the other life is itself an experience. The value of life lies in the qualities which it develops, in the education it imparts, in the kind of man which it produces at the last. The whole great feeling about one man is that he is slipping over the surface of things, merely accumulating marks and scratches on his conduct or his circumstances, and about another man that he is in the heart and soul of things, and that his heart and soul are being inspired and impregnated and changed by theirs—this is the feeling of unspirituality and spirituality in man.

And here is where spirituality becomes religion. At the heart of everything is God. You cannot get your heart close to the heart of anything without it feeling as it lies there the beating of the great heart of God. Go into the gayest and most frivolous assemblage of the city. Stand there and gaze upon the brilliant scene. Get underneath the surface. Realise what these people are. See their souls. Recognise that their souls are not dead, fixed, unchangeable identities. Know that every one of them is pulsating with possibilities, never stationary or stagnant for an instant, changing every moment from something into something else. Let the whole scene be thus a scene of spiritual movement. Be *yourself*, the spectator, also conscious that *you* are a soul full of the vitality of spiritual life. And then it is not so much that God is present there in that room with His children, as we sometimes say, but rather all that assemblage and activity of souls takes place within His soul, within the soul of God. He is not so much present with it as it exists in Him.

There have been—there are—men who try to be spiritual without God : spiritual atheists who recognise the souls of things and their own souls, and try to live in communion with them, and who yet find and believe in no central Soul, the fountain of all spiritual life—no enveloping Soul within which all life goes on. Such men no doubt there are ; but they are most exceptional. To the great world full of men spirituality means God. To live in the spirit is to live in the obedience and communion of that "*Father of spirits*" with whom the flesh is always servant of the soul and the circumstances of the character, with whom the life is always more than meat and the body than raiment, and what a man is more than what he wears or does.

I labour thus to describe to you the spiritual man. But why should I labour? If you do not know him otherwise, no words of mine can set him before your imagination. But you do know him otherwise. You have felt your own spiritual manhood stir ; there have been moments in which you have almost seemed to yourself to be, or to be on the point of becoming, a spiritual man. Then you have seen other men who you knew had made real within themselves that which in you was only a possibility. Then there is Christ, the Man of men, spiritual through and through, shining with spirituality in heart and head and hands. You have caught sight of Him; you know there is such a being as the spiritual man. Through every counterfeit you own the genuine reality—through every counterfeit; yes, visionaries, cranks, fanatics!—men who are turning away from the clear duties of life to dream dreams and ride hobbies of moonshine through fields of self-conceit, men and women who dread clearness of thought and distinctness of work, and the great harmonious co-operations of human life in the directions and ways which the essential character of human life has made habitual through all the ages. These are not spiritual men; these are not men who have gone deep under life; they have gone wide astray from life.

But the really spiritual man is the *healthiest* man—nay, is the only really *healthy* man—in all the world. He wears no badge of his spiritual character upon his bosom, but it shines through all he does and is; it is unmistakable. "*He is not a Jew who is one outwardly,*" said St. Paul; "*he is a Jew who is one inwardly.*" And so it is about this finer Judaism—this which Judaism so crudely represented. He is not a spiritual man which is one outwardly; but there is a spiritual man which is one inwardly—spiritual to the very heart and centre of his life; and he is the only complete and thorough man—nay, the only real and true man—that the world contains.

I call this spirituality the finer Judaism. Where the old Judaism was hard, exclusive, and all mingled with formalism, this spirituality is gentle and gracious and unselfish and free from formality. It is the subtle and celestial and universal fulfilment of that of which the old religion of Jerusalem was the type and promise. And so, to come to what I want you to believe, all which Isaiah sang about the old Judaism, that, small and insignificant and trampled down as it appeared, it yet should be the centre and the sun to which all the nations' eyes should turn, and the source from which the highest power should proceed—all that is true, far more true, of the finer Judaism of spirituality. Is that something which your experience confirms? I think it must be. Tell me, you young men who live in groups in college, or in business, or in society, do you know anything like this : a noise of many forces, rushing this way and that, tossing their arms, lifting up their voices, men all distracted with the thought that they, and they alone, are governing their little world and deciding which way things ought to go; and then gradually, as time goes on, out from behind all these frantic and noisy machines, stealing into sight so softly that men are not aware of it till it is fully there, some gentle, earnest power of character, taking its quiet place in the true centre of the picture, and claiming to be, and recognised by all as being, the true master of it all? How familiar all that is! how beautiful it is! In homes of distress there is a wonderful instinct in the frightened eyes to find out the spiritual man and turn to him. Hundreds of triflers are keeping in some corner of their heart a treasured friendship with some spiritual nature, which in the hour of their great emergency is to be their last and sure resort; as the man conscious of danger keeps his sword ready against the hour when the foe appears. Is there not some man who stands in your little circle, perhaps slighted, perhaps despised, perhaps even persecuted with such petty persecutions as you have to give, to whom you *know* that if the skies were to fall to-morrow, if some great moral crisis or calamity should come, your whole set would turn with an instinctive certainty that his feet, and his only, were standing on the solid rock, and so in him only was there any hope? Do you not know that many and many of the men whom you joyously play with, and the men whom you profitably do business with, are absolutely useless to help your souls, and that this quiet figure, which seems no good to play with and no use to trade with, stands for just what your soul will need in its great exigency? And is not all that just like great Assyria and great Egypt standing and beckoning to one another, and fighting with one another across the head of poor little Palestine, and yet knowing in their hearts that she, the despised and feeble, had in her the true secret of dignity and strength.

It must be very sweet and strong when this Judea-consciousness really takes possession of a man and fills him. It is not pride or conceit. It is something far sacreder than that. But into his ears there comes a message from God : " I have appointed you to help your brethren. I have taught you to see the soul of things. I have filled you with the mystery of living, the awfulness of the soul." Now, "*Behold thou shalt call a nation which thou knowest not, and nations which know not thee shall run unto thee, because of the Lord thy God!*" You cannot picture the soul to which God says that being proud. He to whom God speaks such words stands and listens in complete humility as the footsteps are heard streaming towards him. He struggles for intenser purity, in order that God may shine through him more abundantly and brightly. He opens every door of sympathy, and tries to understand the lots of his brethren, however different they may be from his own. He does not care how far he stands outside the circle of men's *other* interests if only he can help their souls. And when he does see, as he sometimes does, men's eyes grow brighter and their faces full of new light as they turn away from him, he is completely satisfied. Let Assyria and Egypt be as mighty as they will, there is no envy of them in this Judea, who, with no army and no treasury, is gathering into herself spirituality which all the nations shall come up and get from her.

Oh, my dear friend, if in any way God is making you a Judea—if He is using you for one of His gathering and distributing points of spiritual life, *be satisfied*. There is no nobler work which anybody in this world can do than that. To know God so that other souls may know Him from us; to be in any way a deepener and enlightener of the lives of our brethren—what is there for a man to thank God for like that? Do we question that question for a moment? Then look at Jesus! See how in Him you have the very pattern and perfection of that life. He radiated spirituality wherever He went. It fell from Him upon the barest and the noblest natures as sunshine falls upon the dung-heap and the garden. Each life received it as it could, but it fell on all. And more than that, it went with subtle influence to the most hidden lives, and drew them up out of their darkness, to find they knew not what—but something which their natures needed and could not be satisfied until they found. I can almost think of it as if it were a visible picture. I can almost see Jesus as He walks in the streets of Jerusalem drawing out of the great and little houses, out of the courtyards and the alleys, men and women who came to Him with hardly more of deliberate intelligence than that with which the insect creeps into the sun. What they found in Him was *spirituality*. Their lives—

the lives of publicans and Pharisees and Magdalenes alike—grew deep and bright as His light fell upon them. God became possible; God became real. "*I shall draw all men unto Me,*" so He prophesied of Himself. So all Christian history bears witness that He has fulfilled His prophecy.

Jesus was among men what Judea was among the nations. Shall we not think that He was *satisfied?* Can we conceive that He was disappointed because the grosser, coarser forms of power did not belong to Him? Nay, was not that just what was offered Him in His temptation in the wilderness? The Devil said to Him, "Do this, worship me, and you shall have all the power you want to save the world!" But Jesus knew that it was not with these arms that the world was to be saved, and so He filled Himself more full of God out of the depths of His temptation and went His way. Perfectly satisfied He must have been.

And, tell me, shall not you and I be satisfied? God has not given us great wealth to fill our brethren's hunger with abundance, and to keep all the wolves from every door. What He has given us let us use generously and unselfishly, and not be impatient that it is not more. God has not given us vast learning to solve all the problems, or unfailing wisdom to direct all the wanderings, of our brethren's lives. But He has given to every one of us the power to be spiritual, and by our spirituality to lift and lighten and enlarge the lives we touch.

Would you get rid of the lower ambitions, you must be possessed of the higher. Would you escape from the desire to be rich or to be famous or to shine in some of the poor, superficial competitions of your fellow-men? It cannot come about by your killing out desire altogether, and living like a dead thing with not a spark of a wish left burning in your heart. The higher wish must seize and fill you—to be holy, and so to utter the holiness of God. When you have come to that, how calmly you can stand by the roadside and see the great procession of opulence sweep by you with its golden chariots! You can sit in obscurity and hear the shouts salute the favourite of the hour. You will be satisfied. Not merely you can do without those things—you will not want them; you will not hate your neighbour for possessing them. He who hates his neighbour for being rich shows thereby that he has not escaped from the desire to be rich himself. But he who has the power of spirituality has freedom from the vexations and nervous pursuits of lower powers. What should he care for things like those? Is he not sharer of the strength of God? of the attraction which belongs to spirituality?

Do not two exhortations come out of our subject this morning? The first is for good men who are trying to do good to their fellow-men. If you do not succeed, if the real effort which is in you does not touch men and help them, must not one of the reasons be that your goodness lacks spirituality? Ask yourself whether, perhaps, it is not too hard and machine-like and unloving. Ask yourself whether, made infinite, it would be God's goodness. Take it and bathe it in love, glorify it with prayer, get the last unselfishness out of it by consecration, and see if then it does not start to life, and whether men do not feel its power.

The other exhortation is for Assyria and Egypt —for men of worldly ways and hard, unyielding natures. If you do not feel the power of Judaism, you ought to be very much afraid about yourself. If a spiritual life can be lived right by your side, and you receive from it no rebuke or invitation, then *beware!* That is a terrible condition. The spring wind calls to the rock, and it has no green answer to send back. God calls to you by His voice in an enlightened soul, and you are dead. Oh, beware! oh, be afraid and pray! cry out and pray that your life may be rekindled before it is quite dead!

The time shall come when all the heavens shall be full of light; when, as the prophet prophesied, men shall not need to say to one another, "*Know ye the Lord, for all shall know Him, from the least to the greatest*". While that blessed day lingers and has not yet come, God be praised that no star can break forth anywhere without the whole dark heaven being brighter for it, no man's soul can be filled with God without the voice of God to His children becoming thereby fuller and richer on the earth.

THE UNBROKEN CHAIN.

"*But I would not have you to be ignorant, brethren, concerning them which are asleep, that ye sorrow not, even as others which have no hope. For if we believe that Jesus died and rose again, even so them also which sleep in Jesus will God bring with Him.*"—1 Thess. iv. 13, 14.

First and Second Thessalonians contain nothing of argument. Once, indeed, the writer warms up in earnest denunciation of the constant hinderers of his work. This is near the close of the Second Epistle. In a verse or two, almost as if by accident, he expresses himself about the Jews who opposed the Gospel. It is an exceptional instance. In general, these two Epistles are such discourses as one would address to his dearest friends, by whom he is perfectly sure of being understood. We encounter a difficulty in interpretation from our desire to be too systematic. There is here no scheme drawn out. Paul is simply uttering, earnestly and faithfully, exhortations as they come to his mind.

The First and Second Epistles of St. Paul to the Thessalonians were written earliest of all the books of the New Testament—before the other Epistles, before the Apocalypse, and before the Gospels.

No other Christian writings that have gone forth into the world bear so early a date. When we think of the multitude of writings that have gone forth, there must always be something of special interest in these two books of the Christian Scriptures that head the long procession.

We shall better understand these Epistles if we read, in connection with them, the first half of the seventeenth chapter of the Acts. At Thessalonica St. Paul found a synagogue of the Jews; and, as his custom was, he went in and preached Christ. He tried to make the Jews take this great heritage of Christianity. But he found here no welcome among the Jews. His reception was the same as in other places. The preaching of the Gospel seemed to be an interference with the life of the community. It was followed by confusion and tumult. The Apostle was hurried away by the friendly solicitude of those who believed in him, and he went on to Athens. At length Timothy followed, bringing to Paul some account of what was taking place in Thessalonica. He said that the disciples who were left behind had not been spared from persecution, but they had been steadfast in the midst of their sufferings. St. Paul seems to have sat down, his whole soul glowing with sympathy for the persecuted Church, and poured out his heart in the First Epistle. Certain things in the First Epistles were misapprehended, and the Second Epistle was written to correct the misapprehension.

What is the teaching of St. Paul to the Thessalonian Church? We find something of what might have been expected from the working of the spiritual life in the Apostle and in the Church. We cannot read any of the Epistles of St. Paul without seeing how constantly he is thinking of the everlasting life opened to the world by Jesus. He was brought to Jesus by the Divine utterances of Jesus Christ Himself, speaking to him out of the spiritual world. The picture which St. Paul had of Jesus was of Jesus as He is in the spiritual life—not as He was while walking in Galilee. He was to St. Paul not so much the Jesus of the Crucifixion as the Jesus of the Resurrection. The RESURRECTION! That is the great cry and watchword that St. Paul is always uttering. Jesus, rising from the grave, opened the doors of eternity for every man. To the story of the *Resurrection* the Church turns in her persecution and distress for comfort.

The disciples at Thessalonica had taken to their hearts what Paul had told them of the life of the world to come. They looked on the picture with eyes quickened by the sufferings that they were undergoing every day. They saw Jesus in His immortality; and in the immortality of Jesus they saw their own. The First Epistle was written for consolation to the suffering. It contains instructions and assurances in regard to the everlasting life. The Apostle pours out his whole soul to those who he was sure would understand him—those to whom the hope of everlasting life was present in the midst of all their sufferings. He told them of those who had passed already over the river and entered into the life beyond. St. Paul, in the early part of his ministry, with all the Christian disciples, was looking for the speedy return of Jesus. And the question was raised, " If it be so, if Jesus is coming to establish His Church, and we shall be with Him in His Glory, then what of our brethren who have passed out of the world before us?" This was the absorbing question. Mothers had lost their children, brothers had lost their brothers. One by one of these had passed out of their sight. And those who remained said, " What is to become of those who are taken away from us out of this visible world before Christ comes back here?" St. Paul's answer was, that they who remained and were alive should not *" prevent "* *(go before)* those who had passed away. Jesus would bring with Him those who had already died. He would go through the regions of the dead and bring back the souls that had once belonged to this world, and establish their lives. Thus those who had died and those whom Christ should find at His coming would be united and dwell for ever with God.

This teaching had so filled their minds that they began to look for the coming of Christ *at once*.

The tendency to anticipate the speedy coming of the end of the world has shown itself always. When the Apostle uses the term "*we*" they interpreted it of himself and the disciples immediately around him. Though even St. Paul himself did think of the end of the world as close at hand, he wished all men to live as if it might be far away. He wished them to live under the power of the thought that the end of the world was immediately coming, and not yet to grow selfish and heedless in their duties from day to day. It ought not to trouble us that St. Paul and all the early Apostles were thus looking for the speedy coming of Christ Who, in all these centuries in which the world has been lingering, sinning, struggling on amidst doubts and difficulties, has not yet completely come. It ought not to surprise us to find this expectation shared by St. Paul in the full ardour of his first Epistles. In his later writings this idea passed out of St. Paul's mind. He grew to apprehend that the coming of Christ might be postponed for a long time. In all the New Testament the element of time is left out. The Saviour had said, "*Of that day and hour knoweth no man, no, not the angels which are in heaven, neither the Son*". It is not strange, when that darkness lay on the mind of the Saviour Himself, that there should have been a like darkness on the mind of the Disciples. The element of time is nothing to one who lives in eternity and is dealing with eternal things. This great unfolding experience of the world is nothing to Him who sits in eternity and sees the glory to come. To the Apostle, as to other men, something must be left to the development of experience. Some problems must wait for time to unravel them.

From time to time in Christian history the same ideas have come into the Church. The disciples have looked to the skies, anticipating the appearing of the Lord. And the world has always needed to be taught the same lesson—that there is no fixed time possible in which we are to expect the accomplishment of this hope. But this world is Christ's world and Christ is coming into it. These Epistles are the epistles of *immortality*. They have vibrated with rich assurance in multitudes of sorrowing Christian hearts, as men have stood on the borders of life and wondered what is to be their destiny in that state of being towards which their thoughts are so constantly pressing.

The idea of immortality has given rise to the greatest emotions which it is possible for men to feel. It has caused the highest hopes and the most terrible fears. The immortal soul has anticipated its own immortality, and refused to believe in any specious argument that tells it life will end here. Pictures of that future life come floating down into this present life. Men have lived in that other world years before they went there. Men have kept company with the souls there in closer association than with those who were beside them all the time. Multitudes who have doubted the immortality of the soul in their days of ease have, in days of distress and strain, by the bedside of dear friends, believed with a deep human belief that nothing could shake. The heart of man finds its only satisfaction in the expectation of another life. The reaching after immortality has been the heart's deepest underlying root in all the ages of mankind. This world is not enough. We put out our hand, and it falls on one little part of the great scenery; we listen, and hear but one note out of the great chorus. The Thessalonians believed in the other life because they found nothing in this life to satisfy them. We, too, lay hold on the great hope in order to forget how cruel, disappointing, and bewildering this life is which we are living here. And when that impulse rises in our hearts, and we look back amidst our cries and struggles and see the same impulse flickering or else blazing in lives gone before, we become stronger by the sight of their faith.

There are certain questions which men will never cease to ask, and to which they will never find, in this world, satisfactory answers. We wish to know what are the occupations of that other life and the condition under which souls live there. There is only one answer given us in the New Testament—one great, certain answer that is continually repeated—the assurance that souls which have passed into the other life *are growing always dearer to God*. One thing which we want to know about the friends who are separated from us in this world is the company in which they are living. This is what the anxious parent wants to know about the child who is away from home; what we want to know about any friend who is travelling in dangerous lands. The one great assurance of the New Testament in regard to the eternal world—an assurance that ought to be satisfactory and sufficient—is that those who have gone before *are with God*. Let that cheer us. Let us restrain our wondering and curiosity, or be willing that they should not be satisfied, so long as we know with certainty that every soul passing out of this mortal life into the immortal is with the great, true, loving, unforgetting Father. Such souls are in the hands of a mercy that never fails, in the hands of a power that can provide for all the wants of that unknown life. Is there not, in this teaching which St. Paul sent back by Timothy to the Thessalonians, a kind of answer to one of the deepest questions which we ask? *We have here the assurance that there shall be no separation of those who have passed before from those who are left behind. God will gather together all souls, and they shall be together through all eternity.*

Very often the best revelations come to us in connection with some other subject. That question that is pressing upon our souls all the time, " Shall we know each other there?" has been pressing upon the souls of believers in all ages. The Thessalonians longed as we long for the everlasting company of those near and dear. And St. Paul's assurance was that God would bring them who had gone before, and fasten their lives to the lives of those whom Christ should find here at His coming. They who had gone before should come, with all the life opened to them in their immortality, to the Thessalonians who were gathered from their humble trades, and there should be no separation.

We cannot think of ourselves apart from those whom we most intimately love. I may forget the man with whom I did business to-day; I may forget the man who rode by my side in the railway car yesterday. These men have not laid hold on my spiritual life. But that which has laid hold on the spirit is part of the spirit. The mother's teaching to the child binds mother and child for ever and ever. Brothers' lives are not two, but one, for ever and ever. The relation of teacher and scholar, if there has been any real association, has made the teacher part of the taught, and the taught part of the teacher. We know it by the way in which we live continually a part of the life of those who have passed to the eternal world. We are not separated from them now. We live in memory of what we know they once were, and in thought of what they are now in the eternal world. I shall not merely be with those with whom I have had spiritual communion here; I shall be with them as I have never been with them here. The bodily differences will be taken away, the prisons will be broken open, our souls will meet in close union as they have never met here on earth. There are some perplexities which result from the finiteness of our nature, and the impossibility of comprehending the infinite. I have looked in imagination into the other world, and seen it thronged and crowded with the millions in all the ages sweeping into it, and I have said, "How shall I find the few scattered souls that I have known on earth?" The doubt comes of finiteness. Those few souls are for me essentially *the* souls of the everlasting life. Next to the Saviour and the Father and the Holy Spirit, the souls through whose ministry my soul has been helped are to me *the* dwellers in the heavenly world. I shall go to them there as each soul goes to its own degree and place in the life of the New Jerusalem. We come back to the truthfulness of our first impulse, and *know* that we are to be not only for ever with the Lord, but for ever with all those we love.

It seems to me to be the great use of the certainty that we shall live for ever with the souls whom we know in this world, to teach us to live with them now as immortal beings ought to live with one another. If I am to live through all eternity with a soul which has been closely fastened to me in great ministries, in what reverence ought I to live toward that soul now? How should I rejoice in that soul's progress, and stifle every baser feeling that comes up in regard to it? The thorough entrance of this great truth into our present life would reorganise, revivify, and reinspire human society. Then households and churches would be different. The ordinary intercourse of society would become sacred, as the preliminary touches of souls that are to belong together through all eternity. It is indeed something good for us to believe this. Believing this, we shall see each others' souls as well as bodies. And we shall pray for the highest life which it is possible for souls to live with souls. We shall walk together in this antechamber of our lives in such a manner that we shall be fit to walk together for ever.

The Second Epistle shows that the disciples had fastened their eyes absolutely on the other life, to the neglect of the duties of this life. St. Paul seems to put out his hand to restrain this tendency, and to say, "Gaze not too much, too exclusively, on eternity. Look up into the everlasting life and get inspiration; then do the duties of this life with the inspiration gathered from that life." He takes the teaching from his own experience. We are not simply listening to doctrines which he learned and repeated, but to the utterances of the great experiences of his heart. He, too, had found himself fastening his thoughts on the coming of the Saviour. And he had been led to understand that he had nothing to do with the time of Jesus' coming. He did his work under the inspiration of the thought that Jesus was coming some time or other. He might forget the coming of Jesus, and be surprised at any glorious moment when the skies should open and he be found at his preaching or his tent-making. So he taught the disciples to settle themselves down in commonplace Thessalonica again, to endure their persecution and do their work, inspired by the thought that Christ was coming some day. That is the noblest use, the only true use, of the hope of eternal life. We do not grasp the meaning of that hope unless we make it an inspiration toward the doing of the duties which God has given us here. When the first disciples had seen Jesus ascending, the angel said, "*Why stand ye gazing up into heaven? This same Jesus shall so come in like manner.*" And then he sent them about their work. They were to go to it in the strength of this heavenly hope. St. Paul never conceived of the future life as something different and separated from this world. He always seems to talk as if there were but one life, graded as the imperfect and the perfect. Our memories of the death-bed, where the ties of life are broken, do not enter into the teaching of St. Paul. In his thought, life seems to sweep in one continuous, unbroken line, from some town in which a few disciples had listened to his teaching, right on up to the throne of God.

It is possible for eternity to be for ever sending back floods of light upon this life. If we stretch a screen between us and the sun, we shall be always thinking of the screen. We must go to the other side of the screen before we can see the sunlight. But if we take away the screen, down from the sun into all the space between us in comes the sunlight. Christianity was the removal of the screen. Through Christianity the life that now is and the life which is to come were made but one life. I can feel this life which now is to the very end, as I feel the years behind me to my boyhood, as my boyhood felt the years of manhood before me, with their strength. So our total life here and hereafter is not something which comes to an end at death, and is taken up again by the grace of God somewhere else. It is continuous and never broken. Death is nothing but the gathering of the rays of life into a focus, thenceforth to one unbroken life. The knowledge of what I am going to be millions and millions of years hence becomes part of my inspiration now. That knowledge makes my daily task seem not unworthy of immortality. In the dignity of that immortality I do that task.

Sometimes the question is asked, " What would you do to-day if you knew that to-night would be the end of your life? Would you go apart, lay your task aside, separate yourself, and pray, and so be ready for the summons of death?" The nobler feelings of men have always answered, " No; I should go on with the task I was doing— with human work, with helping my friends, only more earnestly, because the time is short. I am trying to leave the world brighter and richer. To do that more faithfully shall be my task this afternoon, if I am to die to-night." Here is the whole rich substance of the Second Epistle to the Thessalonians.

THE MAGDALENE.

"*And behold, a woman in the city, which was a sinner.*"—St. Luke vii. 37.

In this incident in our Lord's life we have a conversation between Him and a Pharisee with whom He had gone up to sup. Yet there is a third person, who, although there comes no word from her, has a true part in the conversation. Sometimes silence is so full of expression that the person who stands by while two others talk seems to take part in the conversation, by continually giving directions to others' thoughts and words.

In this case the company congregated is a significant one. Let us think of that for a few moments. It consisted of Jesus, the Pharisee at whose feast Jesus sat, and the poor woman, creeping in from the street and paying the homage of her devotion, gratitude, and humble love.

We sometimes speak and feel as if Jesus had only to do with the poor and needy. Yet, as we look through the New Testament we are struck by seeing how often He had something to do with those who were rich and prosperous. Jesus was not simply the champion of the poor and sinful.

He came, indeed, to call, not the righteous but sinners to repentance, because only they who know that they are sinners can know their need of repentance. But there is something larger than the mere championship by Jesus of one sort or condition of men. He contributed very much more to the solution of the great problems of human relationship than He could have done if He had made Himself the champion of one side or class or condition or sort of men. Jesus was the representative of humanity, in order that He might inspire humanity with love to God. The testimony which He bore, in His assertion of the richness and the possibilities of human life, was on both sides. On the one side He taught the rich man how to make his riches serve his spiritual life; and on the other side He taught the poor man how to become master of his poverty, and extract from it that help for the soul which could make him rich in the midst of his rags and his famine.

He asserted, in the first place, the way in which a man shall be superior to the fact of poverty or the fact of wealth. And until some such assertion shall take place in the midst of men's conceptions of human life, until it shall be declared possible for a human soul to live in so high a region that it shall be above poverty or riches, the problems of society can never be solved.

Now, when Jesus had been preaching and

healing disease for a while in the streets, He was asked by a certain man to enter into his house and become for a season a part of his household. Jesus did not care whether the man was rich or poor, but He went into his house because he was a man. So He found Himself, for this time at least, at the table of a rich man, and partaking of that which he had to bestow upon Him.

But with the freedom of an Eastern city, of which we can form very little conception, the house was open to every description of persons, and a poor sinful woman came creeping in. Notice that the contrast is not between poverty and wealth, but between two *moral conditions:* between a Pharisee, standing forth in the height of his integrity, and that poor woman, crouching at the feet of Jesus, unwilling, not merely to look up into the face of Jesus, but into any face, because any human face was a rebuke to her.

We must not suppose on account of the words which Jesus spake to the Pharisees sometimes that every Pharisee was surrounded by a great cloud of censure. The Pharisee in Jerusalem seems to me a very modern sort of man. I suppose that is because men, in certain conditions of life, become cosmopolitan, and so are easily recognised by the world at large. The Pharisee was a man of severe and upright integrity. And one thing that had grown in the soil of the whole race of Pharisees was a hatred of sentimentalism.

They had learned that any manifestation of feeling was often insincere, so they had drawn themselves up and said that life was not to manifest itself in any outbursts of emotion. There were certain duties, and whoever did those, in simple, cold austerity and accuracy, should be accepted as the pattern man. They had learned to be indignant at the way in which, very often, men of soft hearts, and not of earnest consciences, had sentimentalised about sin; so that, just as soon as any man fell into great wickedness, or any criminal found himself under arrest and awaiting punishment, these men poured out lavish pity, and seemed to have some sort of admiration for the way in which the sinner had set the law at defiance. We can see the danger into which the Pharisee necessarily would fall. Despising sentimentalism, he would come by-and-by, to despise all the nobler sentiments, confusing sentiment with sentimentalism. Thus he would narrow the possibilities of righteousness. He would come to think righteous only those who could do the things which were possible to the lower natures. The Pharisee had violated very few commandments. He had kept the laws that came down from Moses, and he had added a multitude of laws and had kept these. The trouble with him was that he never had any enterprising desire to help other men and bring sinners back from their sinfulness. His was a religion of hard justice; and that religion of justice must necessarily narrow itself and deal with external things. It was like that which we so often find, the evil that came from a perversion of what was right. From hating mere sentimentality, the Pharisees had come to occupy the position in which they stood when Jesus found them.

How men are always cutting their lives into halves! We have seen this in theology. Theology, in former times, was divided into two separate parts called "justice" and "love". There was supposed to be a certain sort of conflict between these two; and then some adjustment of this by what was called the "plan of salvation". But men have come to think more wisely. We have come to see that Justice, standing alone, would be unjust. And, on the other side, we see that Love, working entirely by itself, and having no deep standards of righteousness, would not really be love. Only that Love which is rooted and every moment exercises itself in Justice, always bringing the threats and dangers of God's law before those whom it loves out of the very heart of its affection; on the other hand, only that Justice which is intent on the salvation of mankind—only such justice and such love can realise the nature of God; and such justice and such love are identical with one another. Justice is but the full exercise of any complete nature in its completeness. For God to leave the sinner in his sin unhelped would be unjust. Love beams upon every page of the gospels and shines from every look of Jesus Christ. Let us not try to separate the justice and the love of God. It is Love that brings us our punishment; it is Justice that brings us our salvation. The complete God gives Himself entirely in the Incarnation for the entire salvation of His poor child who has fallen into sin.

I have been struck very often in looking over the gospels by seeing how many of these oppositions there were between two souls—one of which tried to do every duty, but, not acting from the highest motives, narrowed and restricted duty; while on the other side there has been a soul, which, wandering from God and doing a great many wretched and wicked things, has at the same time, even from wickedness, caught at something of the love of God, and so become fitted for more completely doing His will by-and-by. Do you remember the prayers that came in contrast—that of the Pharisee, "*Lord, I thank Thee that I am not as other men are, or even as this publican*"; and on the other side the publican saying, "*God be merciful to me a (the) sinner*"? We may believe that the Pharisee was in earnest and spoke the truth; but he had no great utterance of love toward God in his soul. The publican was full of sin, but his soul was burning with the desire to escape from sin.

You remember the two sisters into whose house Jesus loved to go. You remember that Martha went on in her restricted way, doing her duty as she saw it, getting the Master's dinner, and making everything comfortable around Him, while Mary sat at His feet, neglecting duty, if you please, but getting the affection of her Master into her soul, and becoming ready for any future duty she might have to do.

You remember the story of the Prodigal Son, where all this comes to its consummation. There is the elder brother who stays in his father's house, and as the years go by breaks no laws of his father. But you get no idea anywhere in the parable that his soul was full of love to his father. Then, by-and-by, the poor prodigal comes back from amidst the harlots and the swine, his soul filled with penitence and love, and receives a glad welcome into his father's house.

You remember how that poor Canaanitish woman, who was in no sense one of Jesus' disciples, had caught a deeper understanding of Him than the disciples themselves.

Indeed we know, as we look through all Christian history, as we look around upon all Christian life to-day, how these two things are constantly presenting themselves. There are certain people, especially in the large churches, who despise all enthusiasm. They have kept the law of God with a certain accuracy all their lives. There are certain other people who congregate in certain other churches, who have come to God out of far wanderings. Do you not know the difference between these two classes? The one class lack enthusiasm; while the other class, conscious of having been dug out of the depths of sinfulness, feel a glow and an enthusiasm, so that their hymns ring through the ears of Christendom, and their prayers seem to go piercing through the ear of God.

Now there is a certain perplexity here. It would seem at first that the son, in order to have the richest garment and eat of the fatted calf, must go and live among the harlots and the swine, and then, out of his wretchedness, come back to the father's house. Some such doctrine men sometimes seem to preach. There seems to be among a great many people a kind of feeling that a man must first be very wicked in order that he may at length be very good. What shall we say with regard to it? Here we have the difficulty presented in the case of the Pharisee and this poor woman; there, in the elder and the younger brother; again, in the Pharisee and the publican as they stood in the temple; by-and-by it appeared in the theology of the Christian Church. St. Paul dealt with it in these words: "*What shall we say then? Shall we continue in sin that grace may abound? God forbid.*"

I think we can see some solution of the mystery, and one sufficiently clear if we look a little. In the first place, does it not seem as if the Pharisee, if he had had a larger heart, would have gained something of the experience of her sin without entrance into the sin in the midst of which she had lived; and so would have known the richness of love with which she came to the Saviour. Suppose the elder brother, some day as he sat in the father's house, and saw how the father's house was sad because of the absent son, had girded himself and said: " I will go and will not rest until I find my brother and bring him back again into my father's house". And suppose that, in the midst of those scenes his whole soul hated, he had found his recreant brother and dragged him home and set him down at the father's table; would not the elder brother have shared in the richness of the younger brother's experience without his sin? Ah! we have seen it. Jesus Christ, the Eldest Son, came forth from the Father's house to bring the wandering son back to His Father's house. And did ever any soul feel the depth and intensity of sin as Jesus felt it? There, I believe, is the way in which a man, without sin, may enter into the depth of gratitude for the rescue from sin, which is in the heart of the rescued sinner himself.

Go into the dark places of our city, find there the men and women who are drunkards and harlots, bring them to the Father's house, that they may be reconciled by the eternal mercy to the eternal holiness. And while each poor rescued sinner will glow with gratitude, he will not be more grateful than you, the sinless brother, who has gone and sought the younger son, and realised his sin even more intensely than he has realised it; that is the way to enter into sin and get the blesing of sinning—may we say—without sin. You will thank God with as true an intensity when you see your brother's robe glowing, white and clean, in your presence, as he will thank God for his inexpressible relief.

But then, I think we must remember that there is no such sinless man; that, however different may be the depths of vileness into which men sink themselves, there is sin enough in any heart to make any soul ashamed and dreadfully afraid; and the soul that is ashamed and dreadfully afraid is ready for the ecstatic sense of pardon when his sin is taken away. Let the Pharisee, entirely apart from that poor woman, look at himself. Let him see Jesus, and anything like the perfect standard of holiness that was in Jesus' life. Then his hands would be lifted in prayer: "*God be merciful to me a (the) sinner!*"

Again, the Pharisee has precisely the same reason for thanking God for having been saved from falling into sin that any vilest sinner has for thanking God when he has been dragged out of sin after falling into it. The man who has been saved from the precipice by virtue of the watching hand outstretched—I do not know why he should not be as grateful as his brother who has been lifted by the same hand out of the depth into which he had fallen from the edge of the precipice.

Your brother has let his life be draggled in the mire, and God has saved him, and he is grateful. You have been saved from all that. What then? Shall you be less grateful for the mercy that has preserved you than he for the mercy that has rescued him? Shall the elder brother who has been kept by the father's love in the household be less grateful than the younger brother who has been brought back again? Two sinners stand together before the mercy seat. If he whose life has been all stained and wretched rejoices with enthusiastic gratitude in proportion to the depth of the sin into which he has fallen, and for which he has been forgiven, shall not his brother standing beside him rejoice that he has been saved from so much into which his poor brother has fallen? Shall he sing cold and heartless songs and have only stunted and crippled gratitude? Shall he not say, "God, I thank Thee that Thou hast preserved me!" with the same intensity and earnestness with which the other says, "I thank Thee that Thou hast rescued me"?

It would be a dreadful thing if the only way in which the soul could come to feel the most intense love of God was to go down into the depths of sin. The soul which climbs the mountain-top and looks at the sun surely ought to see as much of the sun's glory as he who sinks into the darkness, and then welcomes the sunlight which penetrates the darkness in which he lies.

These, then, are the three things: Remember that you have the right and the power to rescue your brother man and share in the enthusiasm and ecstatic gratitude of the rescued soul. In the second place, remember that every soul has sin enough in it to warrant a consecration of the whole life to the God who has rescued the soul, even from that danger of sin in which he has lived. And in the third place that the sense of preservation may lay as deep a hold upon our affections as the sense of rescue.

It is not true that the woman had more power to be the servant of Christ than the Pharisee. The Pharisee who had lived the upright life had power to be more completely the servant of Christ than the woman who had fallen into sin. Jesus looked at the woman and said, "*Thy faith hath saved thee*". Faith is personal. The question was, which should come nearest to Jesus, which should understand the inspiration of His life, which should most leave the feebleness of self-reliance behind and enter into the great strength and peace of being helped of Jesus. Which should it be? Which shall it be, some poor wretch brought back from the depths of sin, or you, saved from much iniquity, yet able to sympathise with him, to see that your sin may be for your soul just as black as his sin is for his soul?

I do not know how much sin you have done. God knows. And God knows there may be men and women among you living your decent and just lives who, in His sight, are just as wicked as this poor woman. I don't think God will say which is the most wicked of His children. I don't think any man has a right to say who is the wickedest man here to-night. It may be, in the sight of God, the man with spotless garments and uplifted head and loftiest position.

THE TEMPTATION OF CHRIST.

"The temptation."—MATT. iv. 3, 4.

IN this fourth chapter of Matthew there appears a personage so much more mysterious and subtle than any of the others whose conversation with Jesus is recorded that the story almost startles us. So subtle is this person or being with whom He speaks, that we sometimes question whether it is a being or person at all. One of the great discussions in theology is as to the nature of the tempter. Certainly we have here an account of something which addresses Jesus and to whom He distinctly and completely replies.

What shall we say in regard to that tempter to whom Jesus spoke in the wilderness? I do not propose to make any answer to the question in regard to the nature of the Devil and the way in which he touches the souls of men. It is some power external to the life of man which enters into conspiracy with something in man to bring sin upon the soul. What is it that tempts mankind? It is not simply the passions of a man's whole life within himself, for continually it is related to things that belong to the world without. On the other hand, it is nothing entirely without ourselves, for such a thing would not be able to tempt us. Any temptation must consist of the union of two powers, something without ourselves conspiring with something within ourselves, some passion of our own nature joining its forces with some enticement or inducement that lies outside our nature. The two together constitute any temptation that really assails our soul. Out of the air and atmosphere around us, out of the unseen forces which we can guess at but cannot understand, and out of the unseen things that have relation to the passions and desires in our nature, come the real temptations to our souls. The will is continually called upon to set itself against the passions as they have been provoked by the temptations that come to them. That temptation comes to all men, and it came to the consummate man, the ideal and perfect man, Christ the Son of God.

But when we say that temptation comes to all men and came to Jesus just as it comes to all men, we want to remember that different kinds of temptation come to different men. I cannot think of Jesus Christ as being subject to some of the temptations that assail our weaker nature.

I cannot think of His being subject to those sensual allurements which attack the souls of men with such tremendous violence. Jesus was tempted in the higher nature in which He lived. And one of the truths which we draw from this temptation is that a man is tempted according to the nature in which he lives. The higher the man lives the higher the temptations which assail him.

Is it, then, that men bring different natures into this world, that men are not born absolutely alike? Is there not some sort of injustice here? There can be no doubt of the different natures which men bring into the world. He who comes of the nobler stock brings the nobler nature; he who comes of the baser stock brings the baser nature. Is there injustice here? Certainly there is inequality. But is there injustice here? See what it would be necessary to do in order that we might obliterate that injustice, if it be one. We should have had to hear God saying to those ancestors preceding the generation at this moment on earth: "It makes no difference to those who come after you how you are to live; you have no power to degrade or to elevate the human stock which shall proceed from you". Can you think what an incitement of good would be taken out of the long history of our humanity, if men were relieved thus of all responsibility for those who come after them; if a man knew that whatever life he lived those who descended from him should be all the same, that it should make no difference to the children how the father had lived? It seems to me that when we think of this, we shall see that in the long treatment of humanity by God it is not possible that God should see all souls sent into the world with precisely the same dispositions. We inherit that which has come down to us; and yet the great truth which adjusts everything is that to every man in his degree and in the sort of nature he brings into the world there come temptations adapted to his peculiar nature. If a man has inherited such a nature from his ancestors that he is free from some of the lower allurements of the flesh there still remains for him the higher temptations which constitute the battle field on which his soul is to be fought for. And whatever may be the nobility of the stock from which he sprang he cannot escape that temptation which the very Son of God fought out in the wilderness with the Devil. He was not tempted to lust, not to those base things which belong to the lower appetites; but there came to Him the temptations which we may believe were strong just in proportion to their subtlety, intense just because they were so spiritual and laid hold of the highest and divinest parts of life.

Think, for instance, what the temptations were. The Devil comes, in the first place, and says: "If Thou be the Son of God, command that these stones be made bread". The appeal was to the God-consciousness that was in Him. Jesus was just in that mysterious period of life when the boyhood is passing into the manhood. Yea, He had passed into manhood; but He had been so secluded from the world thus far that much of the boy was left in

Him. Those years, so full of peril, so full of fascination, so rich and mysterious to the personal being who passes through them; years in which the boy is finding himself a man, and understands neither the boyhood through which he has been passing nor the manhood into which he is entering —these are the years in which supreme temptations come from the consciousness of the supreme qualities in the nature which is trying to understand itself. To Jesus, just getting hold of the truth that there was Divinity in Him, becoming conscious of His identification with the Divine life, the tempter comes and says: " Use this power that is in You; realise Yourself through it; do what God would do, and turn these stones to bread ".

What was the next temptation? The Devil takes Him to the pinnacle of the Temple, and bids Him cast Himself down. For he says to Him: "You are a child of God, and no harm can happen to You". He appeals to the child-consciousness, to the certainty that He belongs to God, to the certainty that the God-love is around Him, to that great supreme and sweet consciousness of His relation to the Divinity, that simple identification with Him and relationship to Him, that the Father loved Him and had great purposes for Him, and held Him in the hollow of His hand. So he said: "Test that which You are just beginning to understand, cast yourself down and He will keep You".

What was the third temptation? The Devil

takes Him up into a high place and says: "This is the world You have come to save. All this great world of humanity is what You have come to save. Now worship me, and I have it in my power to make You such a master of that world that You can save it." It was an appeal to the Saviour's consciousness, the consciousness of the purposes, the commission, the duty that was before the Saviour to Whom he was speaking.

These were the higher things that were in the soul of Jesus. During all His boyhood this consciousness had been fermenting and gradually coming up into clearness. His becoming man was identical with the coming of these three consciousnesses into perfect apprehension. It was to these that the temptation came. How grand that temptation was!

As we think of Jesus looking down into Jerusalem, and seeing the way all base souls there were tempted to lust and drunkenness and greed, we also think of Jesus standing above them untouched by their temptations and yet Himself tempted more than they all.

Yes, my friends, the higher our natures are the more critical are the temptations that come to them. You pass up from temptation into temptation and you do not pass from greater into less, but you pass from less to greater peril. Never expect that a time is coming when temptation shall be outgrown. Believe that by the grace of

God you may trample temptation after temptation under foot; but believe it will be only to pass into temptations that are higher still, temptations that are tokens of a greater nature, temptations that shall make life a struggle on to the very end. Was not that what St. Paul meant when it seemed to him as if no man had ever had to fight temptation as he had to fight it? It was because he had come to the consciousness of diviner things. You say to your wretched and burdened brother: "Conquer your temptations and give up your drink". He says: "If I can do that will everything be bright and serene and happy?" If you are honest with him you will answer him: "Oh no, you are but conquering this temptation that you may mount up to a higher one, that God may prove to you that you have fought a good fight by the strength He gives you for a new fight. And there will be no end to the fighting until the great campaign is over."

Do not think because the grosser appetites do not tempt you, because you can pass by the saloon, because you can pass by those things in this city which are base, therefore there is no battle for you to fight. You were consecrated to a pure life by the very inheritance, perhaps, that has come down to you. In the power of your purity, in the very consciousness of belonging to God, of being a child of God, of having work to do for God, there are the temptations that beset your soul.

I think we want to go on and see how Christ was strengthened against His temptations. I think you remember how one of the characteristics belonging to the answer of every one of those temptations is that Christ always appeals from the false use He is called upon to make of His privileges to the true use which He ought to make of His privileges. He is called upon to tempt God, and His resources are in the true use of His relationship to God. He is called upon to tempt God, and He escapes by trusting God.

Men are always ready, because religion is in danger of superstition and bigotry to say: "We will turn away and live the lower life". Learn from Jesus that the only way to conquer the temptations of the higher life is to realise the higher life in its truth and its completeness. The only way to conquer the temptation to superstition and bigotry, is to be so much more religious than the Pharisee and the bigot that you shall outgrow their pharisaism and bigotry by increasing and not departing from their religion. You are to flee from God to God. Any false relation to God is to be encountered and overcome by establishing a true relation to God. When a man becomes a servant of God and finds himself beset by any of the dangers which belong to the religious life, finds himself growing pharisaical and narrow, there may be the temptation to give the whole thing up and say: "Since the service of God is beset by so many difficulties,

I must withdraw from it and be safe upon lower ground ". " No," answers Jesus; "you must go forward and be more a servant of God." Fanaticism is not the result of being so much but of being so little absorbed to the service of God. When the soul is completely taken into God's service then comes tolerance and charity.

It seems to me that something of the same kind is indicated in the record of what came at the close of the temptation. " Then the Devil leaveth Him, and the angels came and administered unto Him." It was not by going down out of the mountain and mingling with men engaged in the unspiritual things of life, but it was among the angels that he found refuge from the Devil. It is by being more and not less spiritual that the soul is to escape the dangers which beset the spiritual life. One of the things we think of in men is the dangers which beset the spiritual life. It is Christian people who are gathered here to-night. One of the things they think of must be the dangers that come from the very way in which their religion has grown hard and narrow, and perhaps superstitious. Out of the temptations of Jesus let them note as the one richest instruction of their Lent that they must escape from this danger by a larger and larger entrance into the very spirit from which their dangers have proceeded.

Shall we dare to think of Christ as He came back among His fellow-men, and of the things that were in His soul, the things that never left Him? You have been tempted like Jesus because you are a man like Jesus. Have you brought out of your temptation what Jesus brought? What did He bring? A perfect and unchangeable consciousness of God. Had He not heard the very voice of God? Had He not conquered by His Father's strength? Could there ever come a time again when God should not be the very most real presence in the world to Him? He had conquered the tempter and come out free. God had helped Him. The stream that comes pouring down from the cascade, and finds itself safe below, how it must start on toward the ocean, certain that there is its destiny, and it must reach the sea because it has been preserved from the peril through which it has just passed. So the soul, coming out safe by the grace of God from any turmoil of disturbing passions, with what conscious certainty it must go on, sure that God, who has preserved it through that great temptation and trial, will keep it for the unknown purposes which He has for it in the vast future.

Then, I think, even Jesus must have come down with new charity for His brethren. He looked into the faces of the drunken and licentious men in Jerusalem, and said: "I have been there; though in a higher region indeed; yet I know what it is to be tempted of the Devil, and to have to cling with desperate hands to God. I know what great power saved Me. I know the same great power can save them." He helped every soul with an impulse and power that had come, in part at least, out of His own temptation.

Have you come out of your temptation as Christ came out of His, with a profound sense and certainty of God, with absolute reliance upon Him, and with great charity and tolerance and tenderness for all your brethren?

We may think of all life as a period of temptation, and ask whether, when we pass out the gates that stand there at the end, as our souls go, as all shall go, great and small, at last, out of their trials and distresses here; whether the total result of all shall be that we go into eternity with a profound sense of God, eager and earnest in our desire to attain that which God has set before us, and with a great breadth and tenderness of charity that shall make us rejoice when we see entering into the gates of heaven those souls that we have dared to despise and to reject and to think meanly of here upon earth. May that be the issue of life for all of us, my brethren. If it is, no matter when life ends— it may be within a few short hours, or it may be only after years and years—we shall go carrying the results of this life into the world beyond. Whenever it comes, may we have gathered out of this life of temptation and trial a profound confidence in God and eager desire to purify ourselves by His strength and a great love for all of His children for His sake. Then we shall not have lived in vain. Then death will be to us but the beginning of a perfect life.

THE FEEDING OF THE MULTITUDE.

"When Jesus then lifted up His eyes, and saw a great company come unto Him, He saith unto Philip, Whence shall we buy bread, that these may eat?"—ST. JOHN vi. 5.

As we read the story of Jesus in the gospels I think we must often find ourselves trying to imagine what was really the incarnate consciousness, as we may call it, of Christ—what was the feeling which He had in regard to man, as with a superior nature, yet a nature identical with humanity, He went about among men and saw their ordinary life; as, with the intense human sympathy in Him, He sympathised with all that life, knew every one of its temptations, knew the power of evil in the world, and had felt its attack upon His own nature in the temptation and all the experiences which the temptation represented. It must have been a strangely mingled feeling of both the ideal and the real, of what men were designed to be and what they were, with which Jesus went about among His brethren. Knowing men's temptations, He must have wondered how certain men ever trampled them under foot. On the other hand, seeing the divinity in human nature, He must have wondered at the way in which it was possible for men to be content to live in their sins. It must have seemed so strange to see men, now great, now little, now good, now bad. He must have seen men in a certain sort of strange haze of unreality, as when one sees men moving in the moonlight.

I doubt not that there are some people to whom life seems very much like that. Full of the consciousness of God, they wonder at themselves and their brethren for the lower life they live. Then, conscious of the temptations that surround mankind, they are ready to wonder at the higher life.

Men do not all wonder at the same things. Men appreciate their growth by the different orders of things which are able to excite their wonder. The man who lives one sort of life wonders at the man who lives another sort of life. Wonder advances from age to age. The things that men wondered at fifty or one hundred or two hundred years ago do not cause wonder to-day. And, if men should come back from the dim past into our life, they would find abundant sources of wonder at things which we do not think of as wonderful. If we could cast our eyes into the next century, we should go wandering about, seeing things that would appear to us miraculous. The child wonders at things which, by-and-by when he is a man, he finds to be perfectly familiar. From age to age in the life of every man he leaves behind him new surprises. That which surprised him before he finds no longer strange, while new wonders are continually waiting for him beyond. Again, the things that the man wonders at are perfectly clear to the child. Sometimes we outgrow the things which have been familiar to us, and come to places in life in which they seem strange. So every being is measured by his surprises. The strong, independent man walks amidst his brethren feeling all the weakness of their life. The man who appreciates that God is his helper in everything he does looks around and wonders at the multitude of things which are annoyances and vexations to his brethren, making them live low and degraded lives, things that, by the help of God, seem to him not worthy to touch the soul of the man who is really consecrated to God.

Apply all this to the life of Jesus. Can we not see that there must have been something of gradation in His life? That the things which came to Him as wonders in His early life He outgrew as He passed on and became more conscious of the divinity that was in Him? And can we not understand that the things which seem to other men surprises, were not to Him surprises at all? God was so completely one of the postulates of the universe that He did not wonder at the things which caused the admiration of His brethren.

The miracle of Jesus which I want you to think about is an illustration of this. He had passed with His disciples to the other side of Tiberias and come into that region where so many strange things had happened to the Jews. Some of the multitude had passed over with Him. Jesus was not one who cared for the souls of men simply, and cared not how their bodies were faring. When He looked into the faces of the men He knew that they were hungry. There have been teachers who wanted to give mankind a lofty inspiration, but seemed not to care whether men were hungry and thirsty or not. On the other hand, there have been teachers who simply dedicated themselves to the lower walks of humanity. If they could see men well fed and well housed they did not ask themselves whether there was no higher food with which they ought to supply the souls of those whose bodies had now been satiated. The richness and completeness of the life of Jesus seems to me to be shown in this almost as much as in anything, that He cared for the wants of men from the topmost to the bottommost of men's lives. So, as Jesus looked into the faces of the people who had followed Him across the Sea of Tiberias He saw their hunger there. He saw that there was something which their bodies needed. Then there came this conversation with His disciples.

We are especially told that there was no

wonder, surprise, or difficulty in the soul of Jesus Himself. *"This He said to prove Philip, for He Himself knew what He would do."* But the disciple felt a wonder and a perplexity. He said: *"Two hundred pennyworth of bread is not enough that every-one of them may take a little"*. Then another spoke and said: *"There is a lad here with five barley loaves and two small fishes, but what are they among so many?"* Then Jesus, satisfied with that which they had, feeling capacity and power in Himself, bids the men sit down upon the grass, and proceeds to distribute to them that which seems so little, and to make it abundant for all their wants.

Is it not a perfect illustration of what I have been trying to describe? The disciples were full of wonder at that which seemed insufficient. Jesus, seeing the sufficiency, applied it so that it was enough for all around Him. Is not the education of life under the training of Christ very largely this: We mount up from possibility to possibility and little by little come to see sufficiency where we had seen entire insufficiency—a few loaves and the small fishes become abundant when Jesus looks upon them and exercises His power upon their substance.

A man finds himself to be in the midst of certain circumstances, and when he hears any great exhortation from any fellow-man bidding him to live a noble life, or any prompting within the soul, he says: "It is impossible in these circumstances; it is impossible that these few loaves and fishes should feed my nature so that it shall grow into such completion as is called for". So he sits down in his listlessness and is not able to understand that which Jesus by-and-bye comes and tells him, the completeness of these circumstances, their sufficiency at any rate for greater things than he is asked to do. Jesus says: "Let the men sit down. I will touch the loaves and fishes and they shall multiply before you. Only believe there is a greater possibility than you are able to see, and I will lead you forward to the realisation of that possibility; and the little circumstances of your life shall unfold themselves and prove to be abundant accommodation for a great and growing human soul." As soon as the soul has come to feel that not it, but God, is the judge of the circumstances in which it is placed, that same change takes place which took place here. Are you and I, my friends, to judge of the circumstances in which we are placed? It is good for us that we should help our brethren to make the circumstances of their life as much richer than they are now as we possibly can. It is good for us that we should try to improve our own circumstances, and lift up our life so that we shall live among larger things and that we should refuse to live among the lower things in which we find ourselves placed so long as it is possible to live among higher things. But so far as we must live there in the midst of difficult circumstances, let us feel that they are God's circumstances and not ours, and let Him be the judge and not ourselves of what should come forth from them.

As soon as we come forth from childhood and pass beyond the first confusion which is excited by this wondrous world, we look around and say: "What can human nature make of things like these?" Then the wonder opens to us that again and again God has fed souls that were in the meagrest desert; that the souls that lived the noblest in this world have often been the souls that have seemed to live among the meagrest and the most insignificant circumstances. It cannot be that God has sent us into the world to be noble, and has given us conditions among which we can only be base; that God, who bids His children grow, has not supplied them with the materials of growth. In the midst of the meagreness of our circumstances we may sit down and turn from them and look upon Him from whom the supply must come. Then lo! by-and-by the loaves are multiplied.

There are souls to-night mourning over their circumstances and saying: "If I only could be there where he sits in his richness and abundance of machinery and opportunity, then there would be something more for my soul". The soul is taking its own judgment of its possibilities rather than taking God's judgment. It is so much nobler to say: "God set me here to be true and not false, brave and not cowardly; it must be therefore possible for me to bring out of these circumstances something that shall be real food and sustenance and means of growth for this soul which He has set here and which He has never forgotten".

There is also another thing. God teaches the soul not merely that it may be fed through its circumstances, but that it may be fed directly from Him in spite of its circumstances. There is an immediate relation of the soul to God, a personal supply coming from the divine richness, something that can come down from God in spite of circumstances, if not through circumstances; that can make the soul to be fed and enlarged until it shall become what God intended it to be, what God bade it to be when He sent His Son into the world. God never would have called me to enter into a higher life if He had placed me in circumstances where it was impossible. Men living in circumstances which seem to imprison them and to give them no opportunity of escape, men living in drudgery and poverty, seeming to have nothing to do but to earn their hard bread and water from day to day; again and again these men have found themselves, if they trusted in God and lifted their eyes above their circumstances up to Him, have found their lives growing wise with a wisdom that has come to them in the midst of the poor things by which they were surrounded. They have found their souls at liberty, even in the midst of dungeons, and so have walked in spiritual pastures wide, and climbed mountain heights, while lingering in cells where they could scarcely stand upright. And so they have served their brethren as they went on in their pilgrimage of pain.

What shall we think about the world? We look around sometimes, and it seems to us as if the world were doomed; as if there could be nothing in the midst of these endless anxieties pressing upon human life by which humanity could be fed and enabled to grow into that image of God, that Divine likeness, immortality, which is set before it. But even in the most material and meagre circumstances of this life there is some power by which God means to build His kingdom on earth. It is souls that refuse to be discouraged by any circumstances, it is those men who are greater than the conditions in the midst of which they live, because their life is in connection with the life of God, who have laid some stones in the structure of the kingdom of God on earth.

Philip and Andrew will sit down, if they are the only judges of the little supply, and say to the hungry multitude: "There is nothing for you. Here are a few small fishes and a few small loaves. Take them, anybody who pleases; they are of no consequence." But Jesus sees the possibilities where they see no possibilities. So He just goes forward to His miracle, and by-and-by the well-fed multitude go trooping down to the sea again, having eaten a feast in the desert out of the poor little supply—such a feast as they had never eaten when they sat at their loaded tables at home.

I despair sometimes of my circumstances; I despair a thousand times of my soul. What shall come of these wretched disturbances, these passions always running wild, this heart always sinking into stagnation and sloth? What chance is there for my soul? If I see it as I can see it alone, there is no chance. If I see it as God who made it sees it, there is every chance. That is what Jesus came into the world for. Men were despairing. They said: "Let us eat and drink and be merry, for we are good for nothing else". Jesus came, and, lo! He taught humanity a different thought of itself. He taught humanity the possibility of glorifying God and saving fellow-men and growing into something divinely genuine. And the power of Christianity has been that it has helped men to see their souls as God sees their souls, and not as they in their poor weakness can understand the mystery.

"What!" some of you are saying, "do you say that there is a mystery to my soul? What do you mean when you talk like that? This life that runs on and round and round like a treadmill, why do you talk about the mystery of such an existence?"

If that soul came from God and goes to God, if it is to live for ever and for ever in the infinite circumstances and under the developing influences of the celestial life, what business has that man to say that in the few years he has been living here he has comprehended the possibilities of his soul? A man says, "I am thirty or forty years old. What I am now is all I ever can be. I must be satisfied with this." It seems to me that there is nothing in the universe so absurd, we may almost say so blasphemous as that; that a man in these years should have read the mystery of existence which came out of God's life and is to live for ever and ever. It is like a man who should start to run round the world and supposed that he had accomplished all that was given him to do when he ran ten short miles from the home out of whose door he came. Believe in your souls as God believed in them when He made them—when He so loved them that He gave His only-begotten son that you should not die but should inherit eternal life. And then hope opens up before you infinitely. Who cares how slow the growth may be! There is infinite time, infinite room to develop in the great future that lies before us.

What is a man of genius, that wonderful phenomenon that comes here and there into the midst of ordinary life? That strange fire burns so brightly that men look back to it and say: "See what God has done!" What is it that genius does but develop the possibilities which ordinary members do not develop? You have trodden the flower under foot, but the poet comes and looks upon the flower, and in him it develops thoughts that move the hearts of men. To hear the songs that are soundless to ordinary men, to see the sights that to ordinary eyes have no sort of glory, to recognise possibilities where men say it is impossible to make that come forth which ordinary men cannot produce—that is genius; and genius is some feeble illustration, some echo and anticipation of the power that belongs to God, and was shown in Jesus Christ. He was the real godlike essence of humanity; and so what genius feebly guesses at the Son of man, who was also the Son of God, knew. And He said: " My brethren, you must not despair, for you are greater, far greater, than you know, and your circumstances are richer than they seem ".

There is one of the ordinary explanations of the miracles of Jesus which seems to have some truth so far as it rests upon the idea that I have been trying to set forth. What are the miracles? We say that they are wonderful things. Are you sure that they were at all wonderful to Jesus? The man who lives in one region of the world constantly sees that which to a man who lives in another region of the world seems impossible. You go down into the torrid zone and find there growths surpassing anything known here. The feeble little shrubs that struggle into life in your garden there front the sunshine and drink its burning glory into their bosoms. It is no wonder there the way the palm grows high and the orange ripens. Is it not so, or may it not be so, with the miracles of Jesus? That is a wonder to man which is not a wonder to the Son of man who is the Son of God. It is a wonder past all credibility that any man should stand at the door of the tomb and say to the dead, "*Come forth*". But that the manifested Son of God should do it, and that Lazarus should respond to God as he could respond to no most wise magician among men like himself, that is not wonderful. It is not inconceivable that we may come to the time when we may see how Jesus did His miracles, and that they shall be so common in our daily life that we shall no longer count them miracles. Remember always that our use of the word *miracle* is arbitrary. There was no greater miracle in calling Lazarus out of the grave than there will be in the rising of the sun to-morrow morning.

We have only to read the story in order to see where the real power was by which Jesus did this miracle. You know before He broke the bread and sent it round, He lifted up His eyes and gave thanks unto the Father. Every prayer of Jesus was a thanksgiving, and every thanksgiving of Jesus was a prayer. And so it was because Jesus called God into this world, because He made God

His power, that He fed the multitude. It was because Moses, when he struck the rock and made the waters come out of it, called it *his* water, that he was a failure. Jesus, summoning God to be in Him, to give force to that which He was doing, was a real power.

We lift up our eyes, sometimes, before we eat our bread, and thank God. If we really thanked God as Jesus thanked God, He will give as true an answer to our thanksgiving as to His. He will not multiply the loaf upon our table, but He will give strength to the life which that loaf feeds, and the strength will feed our souls, and that is a greater miracle. It is greater that bread taken as the gift of God should feed the character, than that it should be able to feed ten thousand men instead of two. Oh, say your grace over your meal, looking for miracles, so that He shall make that food to be that which on the face of it it is not, that which the eye destitute of faith cannot see in it, the food of the immortal soul.

What is the sum of it all? The man who lives rightly mounts from possibility to possibility. As he comes nearer and nearer to God, God's possibilities open to him. To go forward, so that every day something seems possible which seemed impossible yesterday; so that to-morrow it shall seem possible to forgive my brother that injury he did me yesterday, of which I thought to-day that I could never forgive him; so that to-morrow I can break the bond of that sin from which I said to-day that I could never escape ; so that to-morrow I can lift myself up to a spiritual height of which I said to-day that it may be for other men, but not for me—that is the true growth of the human soul, from possible to greater possible, leaving the impossible behind ; until at last it shall seem to us not impossible that in the long development of the endless eternity we shall some day come to be perfect, "*even as our Father which is in heaven is perfect*".

LESSONS FROM THE LIFE OF JESUS.

"Unto you is born this day in the city of David a Saviour."—St. Luke ii. 10.

CHRISTMAS Day on one side and Good Friday on the other limit and define the active working life of Jesus on the earth. Christmas marks its beginning and Good Friday marks its close. Standing on the height of either of those days, we see that life of Jesus as a whole. Its numerous details blend in one picture; and, in the completeness of the work which Jesus did, we see the wholeness of what Jesus was and is for ever.

The view is not the same from the two points. It is like a landscape seen first from the mountain of the sunrise, with all the glory and promise of the morning on it, and seen by-and-by from the hill of sunset, bathed in the tender and pathetic richness of the evening. And yet the landscape is the same, however the colour and light on it may differ. The life of Jesus is the same, whether we anticipate it on the exultant morning of His birth or remember it on the calm evening of His crucifixion. It is not possible for us, with the four Gospels in our hands and hearts, to stand by the manger at Bethlehem, and not see the cross hovering dimly in the distance of that opening life; impossible for us to forget that He Who is just born is the same that will be crucified some day.

That is why, the deeper Christians we become, the more profound and rich in its associations and suggestions becomes Christmas Day. The more Christ is to us, the more this day, which gathers His whole life up and holds it in the light, must mean. Each year, if that figure in history becomes more central, the first appearance of it on the outskirts of history must grow more interesting. Each year, if our salvation by the Saviour grows more complete, the day when unto us in the city of David was born a Saviour must break upon our lives with more mysterious and gracious power.

My friends, my people, I dare to hope that this is true of some of you. I dare to hope that to some of you this Christmas Day is new and different from any other you have ever seen, because it finds you different. I want to hope and think this, as I try on Christmas morning to speak to you of Christ.

Ever since man, the child of God, had been upon the earth the divine and human had been reaching toward each other, and struggling to come together. The highest motives had been trying to get into human deeds. The noblest man had said, "It is not we: it is some greatness greater than us that does these works at which we ourselves stand gazing in surprise". The sinful souls had looked up and known that somewhere there must be pity and forgiveness. The hearts of men had always filled themselves with hopes which they knew somehow the human and the divine, God and man, must bring to their completion. They had been trying to come together. The meaning of history, the mystery of personal life, everywhere lay in that struggle of the human and the divine, of God and man to come together. *At last they came together in Christ.*

We read all that men have written. We think our own best and deepest thoughts about that nature which has so fascinated and influenced the world; and, after all, do we not feel that the truest and completest thing which we can say of it is this—that in it God and man perfectly met? If that is so, then do we not feel at once that, instead of being what men have sometimes seemed to think and tell each other that it was, an unnatural, almost a monstrous, nature, it really was the most natural nature that the world has ever seen? It represents the life of which the world ought to be full. God and man belong together. That they should be separated is unnatural. This life of Christ in which they met was the true life for which the world was built, the life for which the world is waiting, the manifestation of the Son of God.

And yet this other thing also is true—that the

life of Jesus is unnatural. However it may represent the true legitimate attainment, the consummated fulness, of life upon the earth, it was not grown up to in a steady process, it has been thrust, as it were, into the world by miracle ; and so it stands among men as a stranger and as a surprise to those who have not yet known themselves enough to recognise the perfection of their own life when it is shown to them.

It is this union of the feeling of naturalness with the feeling of unnaturalness about Jesus that gives us, I believe, the key to all men's thought about Him during all these ages through which He has been before their eyes. It indicates to us, also, what the future is to be. Gradually the unnaturalness shall pass away, and the naturalness alone be left. Gradually, but at last perfectly, men shall come to see that an incarnation of God in human nature was, to one who could have deeply understood God and man, the event most thoroughly to be expected in the world. I cannot tell whether they will still call it a miracle, for I cannot say what "miracle" will mean then to men whose whole thought will be full of the naturalness of the supernatural. But, whether they call it miracle or not, it will become the law, the pattern, the inspiration, of the lives they try to live. Christ will be to them no far-off, inimitable idol for their wonder. He will be the supreme picture of what they may be, and so the Fountain out of which their souls may drink the water of life.

Let Him be so to us on Christmas Day. Let this be one of the days when the uncompleted process opens, and lets us see the purpose which it is tending to attain, as if it were already here. Let us look at the life of Jesus and see how, in everything which it was, it is a true revelation to us of what our lives ought to be and may be!

In the first place, then, the life whose beginning we celebrate on Christmas Day was, as it went on even to the end, *a perfectly pure life!* What shall your soul and my soul, my dear brother, think of that? Shall we seem to see a splendid sun shining off there in the heavens, and making the dark world ashamed and wretched by contrast in its blackness? Oh, not so! This light is not a light shining in the heavens: it is a light here upon the earth. This Being, who is absolutely pure, is man. What then? What does and must that mean? Must it not mean that sin is not a part of man; for lo! here is supreme Man, and there is no sin in Him. He is entirely and absolutely pure. O drunkard, your drunkenness is not a necessary part of your humanity! O liar, your falsehood is a base intrusion! O libertine, your lust is the foe of your soul! What messages of deliverance are these! What visions of hope they open up! How they transform the sinner's struggle! Nay, how they set the sinner to struggling! For men believe their sins are part of their human nature. *The Incarnation says it is not so.* To err is not human. It is a base habit of humanity, not its intrinsic nature. Behold the perfect man. In Him is no sin. He is completely pure.

2. And, again, the Christ of Christmas Day then and through all His life *was poor.* That fact we know full well. The picture on the pages of the Gospel with which our eyes are so familiar never lets us forget it. There it always is—the humble company shut out of the great caravansary as insignificant people, and finding their place among the cattle; the perfect destitution of all the things which make life splendid or even comfortable; the carpenter's shop, the long foot journeys, the "*not having where to lay His head*". We know it all; and yet, sometimes, it comes back to us with something almost like discovery and surprise. Was it then true? Did that which all men are accepting as the pattern life come into the world, and go out of the world, without a single sign of any care about those things which the great mass of men are struggling after as if there could be no joy in life without them?

Let a stranger come here, and see our business world. Let him walk through our business streets, and be told that this is a Christian city and these are Christian men. Let him watch their anxious faces. Let him listen to their feverish talk. Let him read the bulletins which they are devouring with hungry eyes. Let him get thoroughly into the soul of this determined, furious pursuit of wealth, and then let him suddenly be told that the great Master of these men, He after whose name almost all of them want to be called, never had any and never wanted to have any of this wealth, to the pursuit of which all these men's lives are given; must he not be surprised? Ah! how vulgar and poor it makes the hunt for money seem! How it ought to break some of these heavy chains! It is not necessary that you should be rich. There is no need of it whatever. Behold! He who struck the highest, purest note of human life, He who showed God to man, He who brought man to God, He who redeemed the world—*He was not rich, but poor.* Oh, blessed fact! What if it had been a rich man that had saved the world? How, conspiring with all man's native passion to be rich, the sight of the rich Redeemer would have enlisted all our best ambitions in the struggle for the money which must then have come to seem indispensable for the best life and work! How terrible that would have been! Heaven and hell almost confederate to make the soul of man the slave of gold But, now, how different! Now, the life of Christ may be misread into a false glorification of poverty, but it never can be made to preach cupidity. Now, he who reads the story of Christ's life knows that to be rich is not, and never can be, the worthy object of a human life. He who reads that story despises his own passion for money. He feels dropping out of his heart the base and brutal contempt for the poor man. And the poor man himself fills his soul with self-respect and strength beside the cradle of the poor Jesus. Oh, my dear friends! is it not true that poor and rich, in themselves and toward each other, can never be what they ought to be so long as to both money seems to be the one desirable thing of life? If that be so, must not the first leaf from the tree which is for the healing of the nations come in this fact that the Son of man—the Man of men, the Man who lived the richest life this world has ever seen —was born and lived and died in poverty?

3. Again, the life of Jesus was *a life of absolute unselfishness*. That means much more than we are apt to make it mean. It means, not merely that a man of generous impulses was often ready to step aside from his own purposes to serve the purposes of others: it means that there is here a man who has a clear and noble and consistent plan of living, and that in that plan of living He Himself is recognised as being not an end, but a means. His own life, even His own character, never seems to Him the final purpose of His living. He lives for others; most of all He lives for God. Now, just think how selfishness, from its lowest to its highest manifestations, rules men's

lives. All the way up, from the poor brute who cannot deny himself the pleasure which his drink will give him, to the scholar who draws his study curtains close and shuts out the sights and sounds of misery, and buries himself in his books—all the way from the brute to the scholar reigns one idea of life. Self-indulgence in some gross or glorious form is the controlling law. "Take care of yourself!" What different things that may mean! But, in some meaning of it, how all men are saying it to their own souls or to one another! The prudent father to his careless son, the teacher to his scholar, old wisdom to young folly, the old year to the new year—everywhere and always it is, "Take care of yourself!" And then —oh, how strange and bewildering it seems sometimes!—there comes into this world of men taking care of themselves the Man; and, behold! He takes no care of Himself. The whole notion of developing Himself, of making Himself this or that, will not fit itself to Him for a moment. He is here solely and purely for these brethren of His. He takes His life, and casts it down before them and bids them walk over it with their rude feet into the life they cannot reach except through Him. True, He is able to catch sight, beyond that humiliation and sacrifice, of a fulfilment and enrichment which are coming to Him by it. His spiritual insight sees and His perfect honesty will not deny, that this losing of His life is to be the saving of it in the end; but that is not—no one who comes in contact with Him dreams for a moment that that is—the purpose for which the life is cast into the dust. Our modern notion of self-culture is not within the mind of Christ. "GLORY OF GOD," "SERVICE OF MAN"—those were the watchwords of His life.

What shall we say? Are there not scores of men and women living lives of discontentment, which are always tending to become lives of self-reproach, because the culture which is within the reach of others is not within their reach? Some hard, absorbing work consumes their time, and early life for them was so burdened with poverty that they had no chance of entering those sacred doors of learning which can be entered only by the fresh and buoyant feet of youth. Will it be nothing, will it not be everything, for them to know that the Greatest of all human beings lived not for culture, but for service? What He lived for is perfectly within their grasp —nay, it is crowding itself upon them all the time—the opportunity of unselfishly glorifying God, of unselfishly serving man.

And here must come the true antidote to all the tendencies of artificial, affected, and false culture which all of you who live in the world which seeks for culture cannot help recognising and fearing. They all spring from the root of selfishness. The Spirit of the Christ who was what He was, not for Himself, but for His brethren—that is the only hope of salvation for it all. "*For their sakes I sanctify Myself,*" these great words of unselfishness, inspiring the sublimest self-cultivation, one would rejoice to see written in gold on the walls of every study and class-room and school-house of the land.

4. Only one thing more let me bid you think of about this life whose beginning we are celebrating now. It was *a very short life*. It had hardly more than begun when it was cut off by a murder. We complain that life is short. We say, "if we had only time, we would do something". The old man, feeling the ground crumbling beneath his feet, struggles almost frantically against the inevitable doom. "Give me a few more years of solid foothold! I am not ready to go yet, I have done nothing. I have had no time. I was just going to begin." Behold, here, what a very bit of a life it was that saved the world! See how the soul of Jesus just touched the earth, and left it burning for ever with new fire. It is not time you want, but *fire*. The cloud lies on the mountain top all day, and leaves it at last just as it found it in the morning, only wet and cold. The lightning touches the mountain for an instant, and the very rocks are melted and the whole shape of the great mass is changed. Oh, most of our lives are long enough! Enough, enough of this which makes up what we call our living! Enough of this

dawdling and loun ing, enough of this chasing of pleasure which we never catch, this thinking idle thoughts which come to nothing, this dreading of dangers which we know not how to avoid! Who would not cry out to God: Oh, make my life how short I care not, so that it can have the fire in it for an hour! If only it can have intensity! Let it but touch the tumult of this world only for an instant! Then let it go, and leave its power behind.

Once or twice in our lives we have stood by the grave-sides of young men which were too solemn for complaint or regret. We were sure that it was right for them to go, after the short, sharp, glorious work they had done. . We could scarcely picture them to ourselves as living to grow old. We saw caught upon their lives the light which came from Christ's, the light which makes it clear that life need.not be long if only it is thoroughly alive.

This, then, is the Christ who comes to us once more on a new Christmas Day. He is the Christ who shows that a human life is all the more human if it be free from sin—the Christ who proclaims unselfishness—the Christ to whom length of life is not necessary, and who plucks the sceptre out of the hand of Death. O my friends, is not this the Christ we need? Is not this the Christ the world needs everywhere? Let Him come to the world and be its Master, and what new life He will bring to all kinds of souls! Let Him come to the young, and He will make them know how free for every good exertion is the world which they are entering. Let Him come to the old, and the world which has begun to grow stale and weary shall clothe itself anew with radiant freshness, shall show itself what it really is—the world of God, which stops with no one of the fleeting generations of His children, but goes on by Him and in Him and into Him deeper and deeper, age after age. Let this Christ we have described come to the rich, and they grow humble. Let Him come to the poor, and they grow brave. Let Him come to the tempted, and they become strong by a strength which is not their own, but which enters into them more deeply than any strength which they have called their own could do. Let Him come to the sorrowful, and sorrow itself, still being sorrow, not casting away its sacredness which is bound up with its love, is filled with solemn and mysterious joy. Let Him come to the dying—yes, let this birth come to death—and it must change death or reveal death to itself as what it is—not an end, but a beginning, not death, but birth itself!

Can Christ, the Christ of Christmas Day, so come to us? Ah! my dear friends, that is not the question. He has come! He is here now! He has been here ever since the great mysterious event which this day celebrates. The question is not whether He can come to us. *He has come!* Now, can we come to Him? Can we break down or overleap whatever barrier stands between His soul of love and us? Can we sweep off the little petty scepticism which we have nursed, of which perhaps we have been proud, and which has kept us from the great richness of faith which lies waiting for our souls beyond? Can we repent anew of the sin which has made this past year tragic and terrible, and take Christ's forgiveness just as freely as He gives it, and be new men hereafter—soberer, humbler men, as those must be who have taken Christ's mercy, and given up themselves entirely to Him.

It is possible on this day, when Christ is born anew to us, for us to be born anew to Him. The Christmases come and go, and each one brings us nearer to the day when we shall see Him face to face. Whether that day be far away or near, He knows; and that is quite enough for us. We will not ask about that, but only pray that we may see Him now, and give ourselves to Him, and let Him make us His and make Himself ours by His grace.

THE TRUE TEST.

"Forbid him not."—St. Luke ix. 49, 50.

THESE words contain but a single remark of Jesus made in response to a single statement of His disciple. It is not easy to set before ourselves the whole circumstances and to understand exactly all the conditions in which any of our Lord's conversations took place. We feel more and more as we read the Gospels how much we must confess ourselves ignorant of the special conditions in which Jesus and His disciples were living; and yet we can more and more clearly perceive the tenor of what the Saviour said. There are very few of His words indeed that are not intelligible to us.

What was meant definitely by casting out devils we cannot understand. It is some distinct and subtle recognition of the way in which the sufferings of this poor human body are bound up with the spiritual life. Some form of pestilence or disease or insanity seems to have been alluded to in this phrase. Nor do we know what was being done when John, as he said, saw a man casting out devils in the name of Jesus Christ. But we can make out very clearly what John meant in what he said to Jesus and what Jesus meant in the answer which He made to John.

Jesus was here dealing with that hardest condition, in which wrong and right are mixed together. It is easy enough to deal with those who are good, to praise those who are doing the commandments of God and walking in His ways. It is easy, on the other hand, to condemn those who are altogether wrong. But it is one of the most interesting things in studying the life of Jesus to see how He dealt with His disciples, who were loyal to Him, and yet were constantly going astray. They had in them a spiritual life, but it was constantly mixed up with very human elements. They were partly right and partly wrong. Jesus had to praise part and condemn part—to weed away the tares and to allow the wheat to stand forth in full beauty.

There was something good and something evil on this occasion. There was good in their jealousy for Him, even though it misled them. There was evil in the narrowness into which it led them. It was that narrowness which Jesus rebuked in the answer which He made to the disciple John. John had met some one who was dealing with disease much in the same way in which Jesus dealt with it, and who was claiming authority in the name of Jesus. The disciples were filled with jealousy for their Master. Knowing that this man had no open and recognised association with Him, they rebuked the man, and told him he had no right to use the sacred name. They thought his cures could not be real and true cures, because he did not walk with the company which immediately belonged to Jesus' life. It would seem that John spoke of this some days after it occurred. Apparently he was led to speak of it by the events which followed the coming down of Jesus from the mountain after the glory of the transfiguration and while the brightness of that heavenly communion was still shining in the Saviour's face. Jesus came down and found the poor lunatic and cast the devil out. That must have brought to the mind of John what took place on a previous day. We can imagine that he had not been satisfied altogether with that which he and the other disciples had done in attempting to cast the devil out; and when he saw Jesus Himself doing the work He naturally turned to Him and told Him of this man whom he had seen casting out devils in His name and whom he had forbidden. And we may suppose that he asked Jesus whether in forbidding him he had done right or wrong.

It seems that there four people involved. In the first place we may think of him from whom the devil was being cast out. There is but little suggestion of him, and yet it seems that he was the one most interested in all the story. He was some poor, afflicted creature, who at last seems to have met with one who had power to cure him. He recognised, we must suppose, that this man was different from other people. He was one who had

THE TRUE TEST.   91

some power over devils. The poor lunatic was thus going to be healed when the disciples of Jesus came and said, "You must not heal him". To that suffering man it must have seemed a cruel thing.

In the second place, there was the man who was casting out an evil spirit. We do not know just exactly where he stood, what degree of association he had with Jesus; but it seems that he was doing something. He had associated himself in some way or other with his great Teacher and Master who was doing such wonderful works. And it appears that the power of the Master was working through him. Then the disciples came with the authority of Jesus, seeming to represent Jesus, and said, " You must not do it ". We can understand his bewilderment. He would say, "Shall I refrain from doing this thing which it is so evident I have the power to do ? "

In the third place, there were the disciples. They had come forward ont of regard to the honour of their Master, and jealous because this work was not done directly under His auspices and in what seemed to be the regular and appointed way. No doubt they were men who rejoiced to see any good work done in the world, and still they bade this man to cease the work he was doing.

Then behind all stands Jesus Himself looking upon the whole transaction and declaring at once, without any hesitation, "*Forbid him not*". It is not right that in this world where sorrow and suffering and sin are so abundant anybody should hinder anybody else who is doing good, no matter how imperfectly and irregularly he is working; for "*he that is not against us is on our side*".

My friends, is it a story of the centuries ago, which belongs only back in the old Book of the Gospel? Is it not the story of what is continually taking place? Wherever Christian men, in very virtue of their loyalty to Christ, incline to limit the operations of His power in the world, there are these four. If they who seem to represent peculiarly the Church of Christ forbid another man who less authoritatively seems to be doing the work of Christ, and Jesus stands forth and declares their interference wrong and impertinent, and tells them to let His work go on in whatever irregular ways and partial manifestations it may be going on, we have over again this picture in the ninth chapter of St. Luke. We have the four again—the poor man being helped by some one who has in him the power of Jesus Christ, the man himself, conscious of some power, not realising what it is that is keeping Christ from a full operation through him; the disciples, standing with superior right and knowledge of Christ and Christ's ways of working, and yet narrowed by their very perception of Him and their loyalty to Him, coming in to hinder the work from going on; and Jesus declaring that they shall let the work proceed. It is taking place everywhere in Christian lands to-day, and everywhere the rebuke of Jesus comes, "*Forbid him not*".

Everything that is going on in the world must be placed either upon one side or the other side. Jesus says: "I work and men work through My power in them. I work through every agency which is pure enough to be inspired by My Spirit." Everything that is making this world better is on the side of Christ. On the other hand, everything that is degrading humanity, making humanity sick instead of well, bad instead of good, is against Christ.

How clear this principle is! Wherever a man, full of errors and blunders and mistakes, but still with the love of Christ in his soul and something of the spirit of Jesus Christ in him, is doing a work for Christ, men are asking whether he has a right to do that work and whether the work that he is doing is Christ's work. It seems to me that I can look back to these works and say: "Yes, and most assuredly it is. Whosoever is not against Him, and this man surely is not against Him, is upon His side."

How Jesus always is pointing us to the great test of results! The tree is to be known by its fruits. The disciples of John, you remember, went to Jesus and saw Him doing His work. They saw that wherever He went blessings dropped from His hands. He helped the poor, preaching the words of the rich, spiritual Gospel to those who were in darkness and death. He healed the sick, He gave sight to the blind. Then we see those disciples going back to John, and John says: " Yes, it is Jesus; for he is doing Jesus' work. It is the Son of the Father. In Him the Father is claiming the children. It must be He, there can be no doubt; whether this is just the form I thought He would come in or not."

In every ecclesiastical congregation, in every Christian Church this must be the test, whether it is doing the work that God wants to have done. It may not be a perfect thing, but it may be doing a portion of the perfect work.

So it is with our personal lives, my friends. Not in the truth we believe, although it is good to believe all truth, lies the real sanction and warrant of our belonging to our Master, Christ. It is not in the regularity of our association with the Church, although it is good to be associated with that Church which He founded and which has come down through the ages from Him. Ultimately there is only this test. We are on His side if we are not against Him. If our work in the world is helping men to be wicked instead of good, then whatever may be our saying or our creed or our part in the assemblies of the Church, we are none of Jesus Christ's. Oh! the simplicity of that great nature which men have been trying to cover with their subtleties ever since the beginning of the Gospel dispensation; so absolutely simple that always it is bursting through these coverings and leaping away from them and claiming for itself this great test: I will be judged by that which I do.

I think it is very interesting that the person who was casting out devils was in some way associated with Jesus and doing it by Jesus' power. He was not some magic worker trying to imitate Jesus without having any of His Spirit. He was casting out devils in the name of Jesus. Would you not think it would have been a joy to His disciples and that they would have said: "He has got a little of Jesus, can we not give him more?" But another principle comes in, which has shown itself in all the ages, the way in which people are inclined to begrudge the activity of those who differ from them only by a shade. Men are willing to see a system, which has nothing in common with their own, doing some good, and are ready to recognise the good it is doing, while some school of their own church, some man who differs from them only by a hair's breadth, is begrudged anything he tries to do. This principle appears perfectly in the disciples. I imagine that if they had seen some one going about with some power which did not in any way recognise Jesus, and doing some good in Jerusalem, they would have recognised and praised it. I think that men need always to be upon their guard against that. I think that men who hold the perfect truth are bound to welcome the degrees of truth which are held by other men. I think that men who call themselves Christians ought always to be upon their guard lest they be separated from their fellow-Christians.

That is our fellowship with all the churches which are around us. We are not called upon to dishonour our own church or disallow that preference for it in our hearts which has grown from long service and rich memories. But when I find that my brother is worshipping the same Christ, although not yet recognising that which is to me of the very substance of my Master's life, His divinity, His sharing the nature of God, I will seek out in that brother's creed everything that is in common and in harmony with mine. I will magnify and multiply that, and believe that so our souls shall both be guided by that light which both of us see, and at last we shall come to a truer understanding of the Master than either of us has to-day.

We can conceive what such an utterance as this of Jesus was to the disciples as they listened to Him. Was it a disappointment that came to them? I think not. I think they were too great and noble men for that. I can almost see the face of John glowing with satisfaction and delight, and a certain release and freedom coming to his soul. I can almost hear him say, "Then I need not have rebuked that man. Then my Master will let me rejoice in every work that is being done in His name, no matter how imperfectly and irregularly it may be done." Oh, let that release come to your souls out of the words of Jesus. Do not think yourselves ever bound to the narrow and exclusive in jealousy for your Lord. Believe He wants you to go through the world as He went through the world, seeking out what men are doing of good and rejoicing in that good.

I can imagine John as he went out and sought the man who had been casting out devils, and said, " Thank God, I was mistaken, my friend, I was wrong when I said you must not do it. Go find that lunatic again if you can. Do that which I forbade your doing."

We are continually to recognise that Jesus lived the life of humanity, illuminated, irradiated, permeated with divinity; still a human life. Jesus valued the end far more than the means, and rejoiced in the attainment of ends that were good and admirable, no matter by what irregular means they might be reached. And only as we come to share in that, only as we come to understand that the great purpose is not that regularity shall be maintained but that the world shall be saved, only so do we enter into the spirit of Jesus and share in the largeness of His comprehension and His life. The object was that the devil should be cast out. The object is to-day and for ever that the devil shall be cast out.

What a phrase that is! It grows as we study it. Again and again the Bible speaks of the devil being cast out of a man. It seems to me at least to point to this; that it is a continual recognition that the spirit of evil is not a part of humanity but an intrusion upon humanity; not that a man becomes evil by some fermentation of his own nature, bad in itself. It is from things which enter into him, a devil which takes possession of him. How precious that is! How it enables us to keep our fundamental faith and our belief in human nature. It is the everlasting testimony, so long as the Gospel stands, that evil is not of the substance of our human nature but an intrusion upon it; that the man who is pure in heart, who has no intrusion of anything foreign, that that man by the very substance and necessity of his human nature shall see God. That runs through all the Bible. There is a humanity at the beginning of the Bible that is pure and holy. When it admits the serpent, something foreign to it, the long tragedy of human history begins. Man freed from all intrusions and made simply man again in the sight of God, renewed in the image of Him in whose image he was first created, stands pure in the heavenly kingdom and walks with the Lamb beside the river of life.

We must understand more what the incarnation was. It was the entrance of Jesus into all human life. The form that walked in Judea and hung upon the cross and lay in the tomb of Joseph, was the presence of God in all human life. And, therefore, not merely in blessings dropped from His fingers, and in authoritative permission from Him, but in all humanity, so far as it possesses His Spirit, there is the power of the incarnation. So, largely, we must think of the entrance of the presence of God into mankind before we can rejoice in all the work that man does for fellow-man, for all the work done in the name of Jesus Christ.

There is only one way in which we shall enter into such sympathy with Jesus that we can have His large Spirit, and that is by catching that which was in His mind, in His soul, the intense value He set upon the end. He rejoices so in the driving out of the devil that anyone who would drive out the devil should have His commendation and His praise, His permission to do it, and His thanksgiving that it had been done. We must have experienced something of the curse of sin and the blessedness of release before we can have such large tolerance for every method of release, for those at work throughout all the world, in the most irregular as well as in the most regular way. Let me, in my own experience, have had such a knowledge of what an awful thing it is to live in sin that I have learned to hate sin, and then let me have had such an ecstatic sense of what it is to escape from sin by the power of Jesus, and then I cannot find fault with any man anywhere who is helping any poor sinner from the evil in which I have been sunk toward the glory into which I have begun to enter. The only salvation from narrowness and exclusiveness is in a deeper spiritual consciousness, in a more glorious recognition of the glorious liberty of the children of God. Seek for that. Do not try immediately to be tolerant, to be tolerant as a direct and special end; but try to hate your sins more, cultivate the work of God, cultivate every spring towards holiness in your heart, and make your life one struggle to get out of the bad and get into the heavens, to get away from the devil and to get to God. Then you will not have it in you to turn your back upon any agency or man that anywhere is trying, even though clumsily, to save any sinner from his sin.

When I hear of men living in contented sin, finding fault with some poor evangelist who, with, it may be, many mistakes, is honestly trying to help his brother out of sin, it seems to me I see a scene over which the angels must grieve. When I see a man coming deeper into the knowledge of Christ's life, hating sin for himself, and so learning that it is the one great curse of his brethern, catching sight of the possibility of holiness and so desiring that every brother may be made whole, then I do not ask whether he is tolerant. I know that he is without asking the question. A man grows broader as he grows deeper. Get down into the very depths of your own natures, understand the great power of salvation, by understanding that with which salvation has to struggle; then look up and thank God that all over the world, in its darkest as in its brightest places, men are casting out devils in the name of Christ. Never forbid them. Try to show them a richer and a better way, if you can, but be thankful for every work of Christ which through all their darkness He gives them power to do. Love the Saviour, and in Him you must love every human creature; and, loving every human creature and your Saviour, you will believe in their power to come together as it is impossible for you to believe until your own soul has come into His presence and received His blessing.

JUDGMENTS OF LIFE.

Psalm X.

In the psalm which we have read together this afternoon, David gives us one of those strong descriptions, emphatic and intense, of the wicked man and the fate that awaits him. One of the things that always strikes us in the Psalms of David is the distinctness with which the wicked man and the righteous man stand before us as clear and distinguishable individuals. We, with our modern ideas and subtle thought, are apt to think of every bad man as partly good and every good man as partly bad, of goodness and badness as always mingled together in personal character. We are so apt to think this that the good man and the bad man do not stand out so clearly before us as they did before David, and, I think I may say, as they stood out before Christ. While that analysis and perception of the weakness of character in each man's life, which is so familiar to us, is very good, David's thought is no doubt the true one—that there is, after all, in every character determination which declares for righteousness or toward unrighteousness. Therefore, the wicked man is distinguished as the man who does not desire goodness, as the man whose face is set away from righteousness, who is living in the midst of unrighteousness, and is content with that life.

I was struck with one verse—the fifth—in that psalm, which describes in one definition this wicked man and his content to live in unrighteousness. David says, " Thy judgments are far above, out of his sight ".

God's judgments are out of a man's sight. Just think of it for a moment. There are regions of which we have no cognisance, which do not enter into our thought or sympathy, in which we are being judged every day. A man's life depends much upon his consciousness of the judgments passed upon him. If a man is satisfied with the lower judgments relating to his earthly condition, which appeal to his immediate prospects, he leaves untasted and untouched his right to the richer series of judgments, which are far above him, and which are condemning or approving all his life. It almost seems to open the universe before us, to let us see the clouds in the heavens filled with the long series of thrones, growing whiter and whiter until the great white throne stands above them all. On each one sits one of the judges, and at the summit of all God himself; and every action that we do, every thought and every life is ever passing up and being judged at each one of these separate judgment seats. And the richness and the sacredness and solemnity of a man's life depend on his consciousness of these judgments which are forever being passed upon him. And the condemnation of the wicked, according to David, is that God's judgments are so far above out of sight, that he is so groping in the dust of the present life that he is unconscious, that he is unmoved, unsolemnised, unchanged, unaffected by all the great judgments which the higher powers of the universe are passing upon his life.

Think how many of us live in lower judgments. Think how we live before the judgment seat of pleasure, deciding whether the thing that we are going to do is to give us happiness or unhappiness for the moment. Think how we live before the judgment seat of profit, deciding whether the thing we are going to do shall make us richer or poorer. Think how we live before the judgment seat of reputation, doing or not doing things according as those who stand around us, with no higher standards than our own, are going to disapprove or approve. And all the time tower before us these great judgment-seats of God, so far above us, out of our sight. Think what some of them are.

The universe is judging us all the time as to whether we shall find and occupy the place that has been appointed for us in the purposes of God. There is no more solemn thought for any man than that there is some one place in the world which is meant for him, which he is capable of filling, and nobody else can fill. And the universe is perpetually judging him by that vacant place, as to whether he is occupying it; and it is condemning or approving him as he does or leaves undone the part set for him to do among all the millions of mankind.

Then there is the judgment which absolute righteousness is always passing upon us, the calm abstraction which we call the right, which makes itself known so really through all the operations of the world. These our lives come up before that righteousness, sitting throned in its calmness, and are judged by it. It casts us aside for our perversity, or it takes us into its embrace, and makes us stronger for what little righteous contribution we have made to the good activities of the world.

Then there are all the pure and noble men who are forever judging us—not malignantly condemning us, not feebly applauding us for little things, but deciding, as each of us comes into their presence, whether there is any use in us, whether there is anything that we can do to make things stronger in the interests of which they live.

Thus the universe and righteousness and the noblest men are sitting on the judgment-seats; and our thoughts and lives are forever coming before them for judgment. And above them, whiter than them all, is the great white throne, where God Himself is sitting, knowing every action of our lives, judging whether we are capable of receiving Him—God with His inexpressible, unutterable, unfathomable love, trying to put Himself into our lives, to make us rich with His richness, good with His goodness, and finding in our character every moment either acceptance or repulsion, either invitation or rejection of His love; God judging us with that importunate affection which beats at the door of our nature, with that affection which would fain make our lives filled with His life, with that affection that feels itself accepted or refused, the judgment of the soul being in the refusal of the offer of God.

O my dear friends, when these great judgments open themselves above us, when these great judgment-seats are filling the sky, and we know that every deed of ours comes before them, how solemn and how dreadful that life becomes—the life which is forever moving toward these judgment-seats and does not know it, the life to which all of God's judgments are out of sight!

Sometimes, you see your friend close at your side doing a work or living a life that is full of discontent. His face grows troubled. The world does not satisfy him as it has been satisfying him. You see that his aspirations are going somewhere far beyond your thought. What does it mean? That he has lifted up his eyes and has seen the loftier and nobler judgment-seats, and that his judgments have come back to him. God grant that they may remain with him until he shall have so remade his life by the power of these lofty judgments that it shall be reconciled to God, and he shall come before them and no longer be ashamed, but saying, " I shall be satisfied with no approval until the universe, righteousness, and the holiest men and God shall claim me for the noblest work that they can do for me and that I can do for them ".

The life of Jesus, what was it ? A life forever pressing forward, forever being judged by higher and higher standards—a life that had peace and freedom from the little slavery and the miserable standards of lower judgments, which stood face to face with God: for there was no judgment of the eternal law, the eternal love that was out of His sight. Not peace: not peace, as we call peace ; not peace that lives in complacency and is content ; nothing short of the peace that is absolute reconciliation with God, that sees and accepts His divine standards, that is willing and craves—nay, demands— to be judged by the highest. No peace, short of that peace which eternity shall bring to us, when having matched the perfect demand with complete obedience, we shall move before the judgment-seat with joy, absolute and perfect ! There comes a peace before that, which is the peace of struggle, the peace of looking forward to that which alone, when it is attained, shall be absolute, entire rest. The peace of the soul which is possible now is the peace of the journey. Only when we come to be perfect as our Father in heaven is perfect shall we have the peace of rest, and the work that shall bring no perplexity, no weariness, no misgivings, but infinite effectiveness, progressiveness, and power forever and forever. In the peace of the journey which despises the sluggish peace which has not yet set out, in the peace of the journey which expects the peace of the end, may we go on in these days, while God keeps us living in this world, to the richer world that is to come!

NOT BEING MIXED WITH FAITH.

HEB. iv. 2.

THERE is always a pathetic interest, made up of sadness and hope together, in the sight of any good thing which fails of power and of its fullest life because it is a fragment, and does not meet the other part which is needed to complete the whole. A seed that lies upon the rock, and finds no ground; an instrument that stands complete in all its mechanism, but with no player's hand to call its music forth; a man who might do brave and useful things under the summons of a friend's enthusiasm, but goes throu h life alone—a nature with fine and noble qualities that need the complement of other qualities which the man lacks to make a fruitful life; a community rich in certain elements of character—as, for instance, energy, hopefulness, self-confidence, but wanting just that profound conscientiousness, that scrupulous integrity which should be the rudder to those broad and eager sails; a church devout without thoughtfulness, or liberal without deep convictions;—where would the long list of illustrations end? Everywhere the most pathetic sights are these in which possibility and failure meet. Indeed, herein lies the general pathos which belongs to the great human history as a whole and to each man's single life.

Not with the quiet satisfaction with which we look at inanimate nature or at the brutes, not with the sublime delight with which we think of God, can our thoughts rest on man, the meeting-place of such evident power and such no less evident deficiency. The sadness does not disappear, but rather increases, as we lift up our eyes to the men who must be held to have succeeded best. From their heights of success only a new range of unfulfilled possibility is opened. And the hope never wholly dies out even for those who fail the worst —we follow them to their graves, almost looking to see them start from the dead and do the thing which they have always been upon the brink of doing. We dare to dream for them of another life, when these powers which the man has carried so long powerless shall be mixed with the capacity or the motive which they have missed, and the life that never has been lived shall be at last begun.

One of these failures is described in the words of Scripture in the declaration: "The word preached did not profit them, not being mixed with faith in them that heard it". Truth fails because it does not meet what the Scripture calls faith. This is evidently something more than mere assent, something more than simple acknowledgment that the truth is true. The essential relations between truth and the nature of man are evidently comprehended in their whole completeness. All that the hearer might have done to truth, all the welcome that he might have extended, all the cordial and manifold relationship into which he might have entered with the word that was preached unto him—all this is in the writer's mind. All this is summed up in the faith which the truth has not found. Faith is simply the full welcome which the human soul can give to anything with which it has essential and natural relationship. It will vary for everything according to that thing's nature, as the hand will shape itself differently according to the different shapes of things it has to grasp. Faith is simply the soul's grasp—a larger or a smaller act according to the largeness or smallness of the object grasped: of one size for a fact, of another for a friend, or another for a principle; but always the soul's grasp, the entrance of the soul into its true and healthy relationship to the object which is offered to it. It is in the fact that there are such essential relationships between man and the things which fill the world about him that the value and beauty of his existence lies. The application of any object to its faculty, the opening of the faculty to its object—that is what makes the richness of all life. In the open faculty the object finds its true mixture, and its highest life begins. You hold a bit of sweet food to the eye, and it finds no welcome there. It is not "mixed with faith". Only when it touches the tongue it opens its possibilities, and becomes first pleasure and then nourishment. You play sweet music to the taste, and the taste cannot hear it. It makes no entrance. It is not mixed with faith; for faith is welcome, the cordial acceptance of any presence into the inmost chambers of our human nature where that particular presence has a right to go.

How easy it is to carry this up from the physical structure to much higher things. You bring a true rich friend, and set him before a sordid man —a man of selfish ambitions—and how powerless he is! He makes no entrance. He is not mixed with faith. You take a great motive, one that has rung like a bugle in the ears of the noblest men that have ever lived, and you make it sound in the ears of a dull boy who has no ambition to be noble; and why is it that it falls dead? Merely because it is "not mixed with faith". It finds no answering manhood in this boy with which it may unite and make a noble man. Truth and a soul that is ready for truth meet like the fuel and the flame. They know each other. It is only the Lord's parable of the sower. The good seed finds the ground ready, and out of their quick union comes the plant that, by-and-by, crowns itself with the flower and the fruit. The seed upon the stony ground comes to nothing because it "is not mixed with faith".

At the bottom of our whole conception of what faith is must lie its personality. There are some things which I can have no faith in, while you may take them into your very heart of hearts. There are other things which I could not live without, but to which you give no welcome. One loves to think of the quick combinations that are going on all around us. Everywhere truths, objects, characters are falling into men's lives, and, finding faith there, are entering on their own higher lives as convictions, powers and inspirations. In one man one truth finds its waiting faith, and in another man another. It is the sublime prerogative of God's Fatherhood that He alone can ask for faith in every man. Only He can stand and look over the world full of His children, and cry to every one: "My son, give Me thy heart". In every heart there ought to be a welcome for Him to its very inmost chambers.

As soon as we understand what the faith is which any object or truth must find and mix itself with before it can put on its fullest life and power, we are impressed with this: that men are always making attempts which never can succeed to give to objects and truths a value which in themselves they never can possess, which can only come to them as they are taken home by faith into the characters of men. We hear men talk about the progress of our country, and by-and-by we find that they mean the increase of its wealth, the development of its resources, the opening of its communications, the growth of its commerce. These do not make a country great. They are powerless until they are mixed with faith; until they give themselves to the improvement of the human qualities by which any real national life, like any real personal life, is made, and make the nation more generous, more upright, and more free. They may do that. It is in the power of a nation, as of a man, to grow greater by every added dollar of its wealth; but a dollar is powerless until it mixes itself with faith and passes into character. And so of far more spiritual things than dollars. You say: "How headlong my boy is! Let me give him a wise friend, and so he shall get wisdom." You say: "Here is my brother, who has been frivolous. Behold, a blessed sorrow is gathering about him, and out of the darkness he will come with a sober heart!" You say: "This man is coarse and brutish; let me set him among fine things, and he will become delicate and gentle". You say: "This selfish creature, who has not cared for his country in what seemed her soft and easy days, let the storm come, let the war burst out or the critical election, big with disgrace or honour, rise up like a sudden rock out of the calm sea, and patriotism will gather at his heart and set his brain to lofty thoughts and strengthen his arm for heroic deeds". Forever the same anticipations from mere circumstances, the same trust in mere emergencies, in facts and things, and forever the same disappointment, forever the same reiterated answer from all experience—like the perpetually-repeated answer that the moaning rock gives to the querulous tide which is always creeping back to hear it once again —the answer that no crisis, no event, no fact, no person is of real value to the soul of any man unless it really gets into that soul, compels or wins its welcome, and passes, by the mixture of faith, into character. So, and so only, does a wise friend make your boy wise, or sorrow make your brother noble, or fine and gentle circumstances make the coarse man fine, or the need of his country make a selfish man a patriot.

Now, all this is peculiarly true with reference to religion. Think how it runs through the Bible. Remember the course of the sacred history, which is a perpetual parable of that other no less sacred history which is the life of every religious man. The story of the Bible is the record of God, who is the great eternal circumstance, the vast surrounding element which always encompasses the life of man, constantly offering Himself to that life and testing its capacity to receive Him. At the beginning comes the mysterious story of Genesis. The Creator walks with the new humanity among the trees of the new garden. But the humanity, as yet unripened by experience, untrained by suffering, unenlightened by the sense of its own essential feebleness, self-confident and superficial, cannot take the Divine society into his deepest heart. Adam and Eve, the young and untrained Earth and Life, take God into the society of their happiness, but they do not admit Him into the inmost chambers, into the government of their wills, and the consolation of their sorrow. At the other end of the Bible is the New Jerusalem, and there what have we? Man, rich in all the fearful and beautiful experience of life; humanity, with all its history of grief and comfort, of sin and redemption—humanity mellowed, softened, humbled, deepened by all the experience of the long, slow day in which the ages of human history have been the creeping hours. And, lo! in this beaten and ripened humanity the doors are all wide open. Even in the deepest chambers enters the ever-present God, and finds in each chamber a new faith, with which He mixes Himself, and becomes the soul's life. "The throne of God and of the Lamb shall be in it; and His servants shall serve Him; and His name shall be in their foreheads." Between the two there is the story of God's perpetual offer of Himself to the soul of man, and of His entrance into it just as far as He finds faith to welcome Him. Noah, Abraham, Moses, David, the Prophets, John the Baptist, Nicodemus, John the Disciple, Paul—each marks some access of the Divine presence to our human life, and each bears witness how impossible it is even for God to enter into a humanity that has not faith, to enter any humanity farther than that humanity has faith to take His blessed presence in.

There is indeed another truth which often mingles with this and softens the harshness which would be in it if it stood alone. That other truth is that every approach of God to man has a true tendency to *make* faith, without which the approach can never become a real entrance. As the face of your unforgotten friend coming towards you reclaims you for himself, and has a true power to make you give that welcome to his love which still at the last nothing but your own willing love can give, and without which he, love you as warmly as he may, cannot enter: so the first truth of religion always must be that there is such an essential and original belonging between God and man, that as God comes to man He makes, as far as any power outside the man's own will can make, the faith which is to be His welcome. If this were not true, life would be very dark and hope would be a mockery. Yet still the truth remains that only into faith, only into a fitness and receptivity of soul, can even God come with His blessed presence. And if it is true of God, it is true certainly of every truth of God, and of all the forms of sacred influence which His presence takes. They cannot enter the real life of a man until they are "mixed with faith".

Just think how this convicts of superficialness a very large part of our labour and expectation for the extension of religion and the benefit of man. We put confidence in our organisations : let us plant our church in this remote village ; let our beloved liturgy be heard among these unfamiliar scenes ; let the episcopate bloom in the far West, and so men shall be saved. It is not so much that we have too much confidence, as that we have the wrong kind of confidence in the objective truth. " Let this which I know is verity come to this bad man's life, and he must turn." There is all about us this faith in the efficacy of ideas over character. The orthodox man believes that if you could silence all dissent from the old venerated creed the world would shine with holiness. The unbeliever thinks that if you could tear the old creeds altogether out of the belief of men, the crushed, creed-ridden heart of man would spring up and enthusiastically claim its privilege of goodness. How like it all sounds to the cry we hear in the parable coming forth from the still unenlightened ruin of a wasted life : " Nay, Father Abraham ; but if one went unto them from the dead they will repent ! " Ideas are mighty. There is no real strength in the world that has not an idea at its heart. To declare true ideas, to speak the truth to men, is the noblest work that any man can covet or try to do. To attempt to gain power over men which shall not be the power of an idea is poor, ignoble work. But yet it is none the less certain that no man really does tell the truth to other men who does not always go about remembering that truth is not profitable till it is mixed with faith, that the final power of acceptance or rejection lies in the soul. It is the forgetfulness of this which has made the useless teachers of every kind, the dreary books, the teachers from whom the scholars have gone away unfed, the faithful but fruitless ministers, the disappointed, unsuccessful missionaries.

But we must go farther than this. The mind of man is far too delicate and sensitive for anything unappropriated and not made a part of itself to be in it without doing it harm. Everything that is there must enter into some relation with the humanity which holds it, and if the relationship be not one of fellowship and help will certainly be hostile and injurious. How universal is this necessity! The person whom a man has studied and understood, but has not learned to sympathise with and love, becomes an irritation, all the more irritating as his life is pressed more closely on the unsympathetic and unloving heart. His motives are distorted; his excellencies excite jealousy instead of admiration; his failings are exaggerated, and make you glad instead of sorry. And so it is of books. The book which you have studied, but whose heart you have not taken into your heart, makes you not a wise man, but a pedant. And so it is with institutions. The government under which you live, but with whose ideas you are not in loyal sympathy, chafes and worries you, and makes you often all the more rebellious in your heart the more punctiliously obedient you are in outward action. And so especially it is in all that pertains to religion. What is the root and source of bigotry, and of that which goes with bigotry —partisanship? The desire that a belief, whether the belief be true or false, should prosper and prevail, not because it is true, but because it is ours. Is not the real reason of these morbid substitutes for healthy belief always this—that truth has been received but not "mixed with faith," not deeply taken into the very nature of the man who has received it? Take any truth—the truth for instance, of the Lord's incarnation. Let it be simply a proved fact to a man, and how easily he makes it the rallying cry of a sect; how easily he comes to hate with personal hatred the men who do not hold it; how ready he is to seek out and magnify the shades of difference in the statements which men make of it who do hold the great truth along with him! But let that same truth be "mixed with faith," let it enter into the depths of a man's nature where it is capable of going, let it awaken in him the deep, clear sense of the unutterable love of God, let it reveal to him his human dignity, his human responsibility, his human need, and then how impossible it will be for him to be a bigot! How all men, believers and unbelievers alike, will be seen by him within the glory of his truth! How he will pity the men who do not know it; how he will welcome and rejoice in any half-knowledge of it, any guess that he sees men making at it, though it be very blind and crude; how he will have fellowship with any man who does believe it, though the form in which that man has conceived and stated it may be wholly different from his own! Yes, bigotry is the fruit, not of too much faith, but of too little. What the bigot needs is not to be freed from the tyranny of his belief, but to be taught what it is really to believe. The partisan's partisanship is a sign, not of his faith, but of his infidelity.

This is what we all need to keep always in our minds as we read religious history, or look around us at the imperfect religious life of to-day. It is possible for us to believe the same everlasting truth which the bigots and the persecutors believed and yet escape their bigotry and terrible intolerance. But we must do it not by believing less deeply, but by believing more deeply than they did. The path to charity lies not away from faith, but into the very heart of faith, for only there true, reasonable, permanent charity abides.

How heavily all this pressed upon the heart of Jesus! He sat with His disciples at the quiet Passover, and His thoughts ran back over all the multitudes to whom His words had come and in whom they had found no faith. "If I had not come and spoken unto them," He said, "they had not had sin." He looked the Pharisees in the face as if He pitied them so while He rebuked them that He would almost, if He could, have plucked away again the truth which He had taught them. "If ye were blind," He said, "ye should have no sin." How He must look at some of us! The sorrow with which He wept over Jerusalem must be forever newly awakened in His heart. He sees men believing all wrong because they do not believe enough. He sees us taking with one part of our nature what was meant for the whole; taking with our wills what our affections ought to take, taking with slavish fear what we ought to embrace with glowing love. Can we not almost hear Him say, as if He pitied us for the very richness of the truth which He has offered us, the very richness with which he has offered us Himself, the old sad words, "How is it that ye have no faith?" The whole of the life and teaching of Christ is full of emphasis laid on the value of the soul and its personal life. Two words describe the work that Jesus is always declaring that He has come to do for men—revelation and regeneration; the opening of Divine truth and power to men and the making of men fit for the Divine truth and power. Truth for men and men for truth. He says to Nathaniel, "Thou shalt see greater things than these". He says to Nicodemus, "Ye must be born again". And He declares that He Himself is the force by which both shall be accomplished. As we read the story of the men who have tried to help the world, we see the Divine supremacy of Jesus in the proportion which these two offers, these two promises, revelation and regeneration, always held to one another in His mind and teaching. There have been many teachers whose one idea was revelation, and their truth has passed away and left men unlifted, unaroused; there have been other teachers whose one idea was regeneration, the making of new men; but they brought no truth which could at once feed and fasten the character which they tried to inspire. Jesus comes with both, and yet always the new manhood is the great supreme thing. Revelation always demands regeneration, and then its whole work is to complete it and to make it permanent.

It is good for us to believe that many and many a man to whom these doctrines of Christianity are very dark does yet catch from the whole aspect of Christ and from all He says this great and deep conviction of the value of the soul, and of the infinite importance that it should be kept pure and true and ready. That is the beginning of the healthiest process of the new life. To the soul so guarded and so open all truth shall come. For before the faith which receives truth and turns it into power there must come the other faith which knows that the soul is made for truth and waits expectant of it coming. And when this deepest and first faith is really present, the other, sooner or later, cannot fail to come.

How vast a future this idea of faith opens to humanity! We think sometimes that we have come in sight of the end of progress, that we live where we can at least foresee an enchanted world. Our ships have sailed the sphere around; our curiosity has searched to the roots of the mountains and swept the bottoms of the seas. Men have played every *rôle* before us which imagination and ambition could suggest. What can there be before the eyes that are to come when we are gone but endless reiteration of old things? Is not the interest of life almost used up? No! The interest of life is not in the things that happen, but in the men who see. If man be capable of perpetual-renewal by ever-increasing faith, then to the ever new man the old world shall be forever new. It will not need strange things. The things that we call common, the things that have been long familiar, the things which have been, and have been done over and over since the world began, shall shine forever with new light. There must be a limit to the wonders that the world has to show, the stories that it has to tell; but the relations which may exist between the world and the soul of man ever growing in receptive faith are practically without limit; and so the everlasting interest of life, the perpetual progress of humanity is sure.

What a light, too, this throws upon the life which many a fellow-man is living now close by our side. How much richer than we can begin to know, the world must be to our brother who has a faith which we have not! According to our faith, so is the world to each of us. I dare to give my pity to some man who seems to live a meagre life. How few things happen in his day! How little light there is in his dark house! How dull the voices are that break his silence! But who am I, that I should give him pity? Let me know that it is not what he *has*, but what he *is* that makes the poverty or richness of life. It may well be that while I pity him his deeper faith is seeing visions and hearing music in familiar things of which I have no dream. The world is more to every true, unselfish man when he knows that his perception is no measure of its wealth, but that the deeper souls are all the time finding it rich beyond all that he has imagined.

This same truth gives us some light upon the everlasting life, the life beyond the grave. The revelation tells us of golden gates and streets of pearl. It tells us also of beings who walk in them with a precious and mystic name written upon their foreheads. Let us be sure that the new name in the forehead is what makes the reality of heaven far more than the gold under the feet. The new circumstances shall be much, but the new man shall be more. Only by knowing that can we be truly getting ready for heaven here. We can do nothing now to build the streets and gates, but by God's grace we can do much, very much, now to begin to become the men and women to whom one day heaven shall be possible. Then heaven when it comes will not be strange. Only from a deepening of the faith by which we sought it shall we receive and absorb, and grow in and by its richness forever and forever.

LIBERTY OF THE CHRISTIAN LIFE.

"If the Son therefore shall make you free ye shall be free indeed."—ST. JOHN viii. 36.

Two truths I wish to set before you this morning. In the first place, the truth that every man must advance through liberty, and not through servitude. There is absolutely no creative power in slavery. Slavery may keep a man from certain temptations or certain dangers, but it never can create in him the power of life. Therefore the hope of the world is not in deeper servitude, but in richer liberty. It is not by casting men into dungeons, but by bringing them forth into the open air, that the perfection of human life is to be attained. And in the second place, this truth: That every man stands on the brink of greater, richer, and more divine things than he ordinarily apprehends. There are chambers in every man's life which are not open, but which are just ajar and all ready to be opened, on which the touch may fall at any moment. When those two truths come together and force themselves into the channel of a man's life, then that man's life is renewed, and the man is born again. Then, moving toward freedom and not toward slavery, looking toward enfranchisement and not toward greater restraint, he anticipates the coming into his life of the power of God, preparing that life to receive the truth of God; having the great revelation of the Incarnation, that God came into our human life to make known to it this saving freedom.

I cannot speak of liberty without speaking of Christ as the Great Liberator, the Power of Liberation that comes into the human life. And I want to try to point you this morning to the power of Christ, by which He liberates the human soul and sends it forth into this larger destiny.

I am glad to speak of Christ, my Master, thus, because so often in Christendom it has seemed as if Christ were the enslaver of mankind, as if He went among men as He went through the temple, with a lash, rebuking men simply for their iniquities; as if He were continually uttering the great *"Thou shalt not"* of prohibition, telling men what they must not do, and rebuking them for their wrong acts. This is but the subordinate message of Him who comes to us with the Gospel of Christianity. His great message is that of freedom and of a larger life; and every breaking away of anyone from slavery is but the preliminary to the opening of some larger chamber of the human life.

What shall we say, then, when we speak of Christ as the Liberator of mankind—Christ the great Giver of liberty?

We say, in the first place: *That it is absolutely impossible that any man shall give to another man that which he does not himself possess; that it is impossible that any man shall open the prison door from the inside, unless he have the key in his own hand.* But One comes from the outside, from the region of liberty, and opens the prison doors to those who are shut up within. Therefore, when we think of the liberty which Christ gives, and of the larger life which Christ opens to us, we think, first of all, of the liberty which belongs to HIM.

Look back with me to that Figure that stands far away in history, and which, as we look upon it, seems to come down through all the distant ages of history, from the time in which He lived until He is present here in our own time. I do not ask you to go away from our modern life, from our nineteenth-century city, with its great tumult, that you may find Christ. I ask you only to look there, in the distance, that you may see what He was and what He for ever is, and see all the story which is written for us in the Gospels, and see what the power of the Gospel is in our own time and place.

When I attempt to enumerate the instances, the special forms, in which the liberty of Jesus Christ, in that wonderful life of His, shows itself to us, it seems to me that, in the first place, I dwell upon His absolute freedom from that which is holding multitudes of us in some sort of slavery to-day.

I marvel, when I look back to Jesus Christ, turning my eyes suddenly from our modern life, to see there a figure absolutely free from those ambitions and that covetousness which are absorbing so much of our life. *Christ cares absolutely nothing for riches or for luxury.* Do you realise the difference in which that sets Him from our daily life, and yet the way in which it brings Him to our deeper thought and understanding? He cares nothing for those things that we are perpetually pursuing.

There have been others who have indicated to us something of that sort of freedom. There have been noble men in every time who have given us revelations that these things which are holding our thoughts and our time and all our faculties are not really the things which are material. There is always a liberating power when a man comes to be among us and is free from the slavery of those things to which we are enchained; when a man, not by any mere discontent or peevishness, nor by inability to avail himself of them, but because his life is so rich without them, does without the things which it seems to us we could not possibly do without. Have you seen the man here in your own community to whom the things which you deeply valued were as nothing—absorbed in some deep issues of sound philosophy; aroused, enkindled to some noblest generosity; lifted up to the heights of some large philanthropy? Has it not stirred deep questions in your mind when such a man, absolutely liberated, has taken from his shoulders, as though unconscious of the load which he was throwing away, that burden which we are carrying every day—the burden of the riches and luxury of human life?

The wonder of Jesus Christ, in the first place, is that human nature, absolutely and truly human, *was absolutely free from all such desires.* It was not that they are desires that belong to modern times. It was not that they are ambitions that have been generated in the midst of our modern commercial and social life, and that they did not belong to Jerusalem. I think that we sometimes fancy to ourselves that the people of Jerusalem cared nothing for these things. Jerusalem was a great commercial city. It was a rich city. There were rich men in Jerusalem just as there are rich men here to-day. There were men whose desire was to add to their money, to increase their hoard, just exactly as there are such men here in your metropolis now. There were camels waiting at the needle's eye to see whether they might not by some strange wonder pass through into the kingdom of God, carrying their covetousness with them. In the midst of these there walks the figure of Jesus Christ, absolutely free from their desires. I find nothing of scornfulness of wealth in Jesus. I find nothing of any vulgar scorn with regard to the exercise of man's powers which gather around man the comforts of life. But I do find in him an absolute freedom from any slavery to the comforts or luxuries or the abundances of life. More than that, I do seem to see Him putting His hand into the very heart of this desire for riches, and plucking out everything valuable and true, and keeping that. All the noble vitality of man, all the richness of man's intercourse with his brethren—all *that* He would keep, but the covetousness after riches He is absolutely independent of and free from.

Then, when I would go on from that, I find another freedom from slavery in Jesus. There comes another part of the richness of His life. *He is absolutely free from the thraldom of sin,* because life is so rich and interesting to Him.

I think (and you will perhaps agree with me) that some of you could furnish me with illustrations out of your own experience that perhaps I will not be able to furnish you out of mine. I think that one of the reasons why men hold to sin, why men go on in habits which they themselves despise, is that they are somehow afraid that there does not lie outside of that region of life anything that would interest them in vitality. They think of the old phrase that has been tossed to and fro upon the lips of men in all these years, when the young man has called it "seeing life," when he has gone into the depths of iniquity, when he has waded through the mire and slime of every profligate and degraded habit. There is just exactly the key to what I mean. A young man calls that thing " seeing life ".

What did Jesus Christ call "seeing life"? He lifted up His eyes and looked abroad, and life was full of the spirit of His Father, and intensely interesting to Him, absorbing in every direction. There never came a fear to Him lest, if He were not profligate, abandoning His life to luxury and idleness and sin, the world would pall upon Him, and there would be nothing left for Him to do—nothing left for those hands that were for ever being claimed by human need; nothing left for those feet that were for ever being summoned to errands which they could not refuse, in order to accomplish which they must leave everything else behind; nothing left for those eyes to see, when there was the deeper truth of God's love and the deeper depth of human nature for them to be looking into every moment.

Ah, my friends, if there is any delusion in a man's soul that Jesus Christ dispels, is it not that one—that life has no interest apart from profligacy, frivolity, and sin? He who knows the true interest of life enters into the freedom of Christ, and leaves the stains behind him, slipping from his garments, and goes forth into the full light of the freedom of God.

Then, I think another of the great freedoms of Jesus was His freedom from those things which are perpetually holding us down because they are so subtle and deep—*the freedom from the ordinary traditions of society.* Jesus stepped right across the traditions of Jerusalem. And yet—is it not wonderful?—have you ever thought how there is in Jesus not the least sign of defiance? He is not one of your light-blooded people who think that virtue consists in defying the conventionalities by which a man is surrounded. That is purely negative. There was the absolutely positive in Jesus Christ; and because He was absorbed in those truths which lie at the very bottom of all things, He could afford to be regardless of the traditions which had come down and which constituted so much of the life of the men that were around Him. Jesus was the great radical. Why? Because He was truly conservative. Conservatism and radicalism, far as they seem to be from one another upon the surface of our life, come together and meet and are one at the bottom of our life. No man can be a true conservative who has not hold upon the fundamental principles and the eternal truths of the universe; and no man can be a real radical who is not preserving those truths and insisting that in them lies the perpetuity of human happiness and human goodness.

Another wonderful thing about Christ is that in His day He was the disturber of things; but what is He to-day? The revolutionary man seems to see Christ having no share in his disturbances; and the conservative man, as we call him—the man who desires the perpetuity of society, who is apt to call himself a Christian—simply gives all the solid conservatism that is in his life to the Church of Jesus Christ, which was once the most radical and disturbing element in our human society. What is it to-day but very often the home into which old abuses creep, and where men keep themselves quiet and dumb and blind from seeing the flagrant enormities and the prevalent needs of the time? There is the difference between the Church of to-day and the Church of Christ in His day, who carried the Church within His own Divine and human bosom; who could defy the traditions by which He was surrounded, simply because He had His peculiar abiding-place within the truths of which those traditions pretended to be the embodiments, and of which they were very often the corruptions and the misrepresentations.

And so, everywhere, Jesus, as we may say in a more general way, is able to be free from the circumstances of life because He is bound to the character of life; is free from regarding the circumstances of human kind. It is no effort to Jesus when He goes down the Jerusalem street this morning and speaks to the poor man as kindly as to the rich man, and habitually gives to the despised man and the profligate and the sinner just as courteous a welcome as that which He addresses to the Scribe and Pharisee who pay Him their morning compliments. And so, because He has entered into the higher region of men, because He knows them by their character, I can see the difference come into that perfect face as He meets the man who is all mean and base and hypocritical, and then looks into the sunny countenance of him who is so open and frank that he has nothing to hide from all the world. Character is absolutely clear to Jesus, and that is the reason why the difference in circumstances is nothing to Him. And, my friend, you will never, in any artificial way, escape from the slavery of circumstances. You will never escape from that slavery until you get into some such intense valuation of character as belonged to Jesus Christ. Jesus Christ lived in the spirit of true democracy. Why? Because human nature opened itself to Him in its fulness and variety, and He saw men as they were. Therefore no mere outward disguise, no habit in which they walked among their fellow-men, could have any significance to Him. There is no absolute equality of men; but not because some men are rich and some are poor, not because some men are famous and some despised. There is no absolute equality of men, because the range of human character is everlastingly various and different. There is no difference between the poor man and the rich man; but *there is an everlasting difference between the bad man and the good man.* It is only by entering into the depths of moral distinctions, and their profound and hidden meaning, that man escapes from that slavery which cringes to the one and bullies over the other, and makes him thoroughly the slave of the men whom he thinks at the time he is making his subjects and his slaves.

Now, these are the services, the liberations, of Jesus. And don't you see how radical and how true they are; how every one of them has this peculiarity about it, that he who enters into the liberty escapes from slavery by entering into the liberty? Jesus Christ escapes from the slavery of money and of luxury, because His soul is absorbed in the eternal plans of God. He escapes from the slavery of the lusts and passions, because His whole nature is always taken up with the nobleness and positiveness of righteousness. He escapes from the traditions of His people, because He lives in the eternal truths of God; and He escapes from circumstances because he lives in character. Jesus Christ is positive, and not negative. Liberty, and not slavery, you see entirely in His escape.

I love to think of that calm figure, walking majestically, because it is so absolutely calm, through the perplexed and troubled and feverish streets, as if He stood to-day and rebuked you— why? Not for doing the things which you are doing; not for being occupied with the details of life which have been thrust into your hands, and which you have constantly to do with: but for being the slaves where you ought to be the masters; for being ruled by the things which you ought to have under your control. Here He stands, the poor Christ, the calm Christ, the simple Christ, in the midst of our riches and our agitation and our complexity and our artificialness and our slowness of life. Here He stands; and you have come to worship Him this morning. What must it mean, my friends? What must it mean that you rich men have come and bowed down before the poor Jesus Christ? What must it mean that you have come out of your gorgeous houses and have come to kneel and bow down here before Him who had not where to lay His head? Does it mean that your gorgeous houses and your rich luxury is wrong? No, no; but it does mean that you have found in Him something that is greater; unless you go away clear in the sense that He, and that which He represents, is greater, you have lost the lesson of His teaching, you have lost the presence of His life. .

When you have come here, you men of complicated and disturbed and complex life, you have come to one to whom life is absolutely simple. You have come to Jesus who knows but one problem and that is sin; who knows but one advantage, and that is holiness. May not your lives grow clearer, so that many things will seem to you of little consequence which have seemed to you of vast importance?

And you have come here, poor men, into the presence of the poor Jesus Christ, to look into the face of the best that divinity in humanity has to show; and, lo! it bears upon its features the unmistakable mark of poverty. You have found your brother in the poor man Jesus Christ. Shall not some poor man, some poor boy, go back to his life knowing that in poverty there may be every dignity of human life ; go back, not simply respecting his property, but respecting the way in which a man may live in his poverty, rejoicing that those things which he has struggled for, which he will still struggle for, are not the necessities of human life? Shall we not, so turning away from the sight of the free Jesus Christ, enter into something which really shall be like His liberty?

But now, while I am occupying you for a few moments, may I not ask you to think something of the way in which Jesus Christ became so free? He became thus free simply because He was for ever tied to, and for ever conscious of, the higher belongings of His life. He remembered that He was the Son of God.

If we can enter into the company of Christ and live there, then our unknown possibilities shall open to us, and in the light of those unknown possibilities we shall be able to despise and to escape from the baser things that cling to us. Do you remember how He went snapping this chain and that chain among the sons of men whom His life touched? Nicodemus came to Him, and the creed-bound Pharisee became the faith-clad man. Christ came to the poor Magdalen, and in her sin He touched her, and she lifted herself up and was free, not only from her sin, but from the tyranny of her dark remorse, and entered into His service, and by-and-by was with Him at His crucifixion. He came to twelve plain men, plainer than almost any man that is in this house to-day, and touched their lives, and each and every one of those men became that which any one of us would give his life if he could become—one of the Apostles of the new redemption, one of the saviours of the world.

Ah, my friends, it must be a personal following of a personal leader. A creed can never make me believe how wonderful man is, how wonderful I am. It may tell it to me, and the words bound back again from my intelligence on which they strike. A rite or a ceremony can never, in itself, force it any farther than my fingers and my mouth. But the Master, the personal manifestation of it, the Christ who is to-day that which He has been in all the ages, He who walks so humble and so strong, so free because of His absorption, devotion, and consecration to His Father—He brings it to me. And if you will let Him walk with you in your streets, and sit with you in your offices, and be with you in your homes, and teach you in your churches, and abide with you as the Living Presence in your hearts, you, too, shall know what freedom is, and, while you do your duties, be above your duties; and while you live your life, still walk, already walk, in heaven; and, while you own yourselves the sons of men, know that you are the sons of God.

IMMORTALITY.

In that He died, He died unto sin once; but in that He liveth, He liveth unto God.—ROMANS vi. 10.

IT is the beauty and the glory of the great festivals of the Christian Church that they bring us into the immediate presence of the most solemn and infinite ideas. It is possible to treat them in a very small and meagre way, as occasions for great assemblies and splendid decorations. But if we get at the heart of them they bring us into the presence of some world-wide, universe-wide ideas, and compel us to face the solemn facts of our existence. It is not that we have forgotten these truths, but that we need to be brought again and again into their spirit. They strike the key-note of our humanity, and make us remember what a large and glorious thing it is to live in our human life. How good it is that Christmas-day and Easter Sunday, and the other great festivals of the Christian year, bring back to us the great truths of our humanity, and we remember that to be children of God is indeed an infinite and glorious privilege.

You have assembled, and multitudes in all our churches have assembled—for what? Let us get at the very heart and root of it. It is that we may remember that we are immortal. You know the story of the monarch who looked abroad on the multitudes in his armies, and turned away and wept as he reflected that, when a few years should have passed away, not one of those upon whom he was looking would remain in the earth. May we not look abroad on such an assemblage as this gathered here to-day and think with exultation and joy that after ages upon ages shall have passed, every one, the most insignificant as well as the greatest, the greatest as well as the most insignificant, of this assembly here will still be living, going forward in the same identical human career, developing the same humanity, finding the same humanity capable of infinite development, just as we are living here upon this Easter morning? Whatever motive brought you here on this Easter morning, lift up your hearts for a few moments in face of the fact of your immortality and think what it is and what it means that you are to live for ever and for ever.

The world did believe before the first Easter day in immortality and the resurrection from the dead; and yet there came a time when that truth was especially manifested; and that time was the first Easter-day. It is the glory of that day, of the resurrection of Christ, and always has been, that it was the manifestation of the truth which men did believe in their hearts in many loftiest moods and moments. Just as the fire that is beneath the crust of the globe bursts forth here and there in the volcano, so the nobler qualities of human life, which are always present even in the weakest of human beings, shine forth here and there in superb deeds, and men become aware not only of what a few great men have done, but what it is in their own souls to do. The resurrection of Jesus, the Son of Man, is the completion and crown of our humanity. The second Adam bore witness to the glory, the power of a resurrection, that is in every human life. The first Adam bore witness to the weakness and wretchedness in mankind. Man looked back to Genesis and recognised himself there, and knew that he was capable of that which is recorded in the far distant gloom of the garden of Eden. But man, reading the story of the first resurrection, has always recognised himself there, too, and known that he was capable of the same conquest over sin and death and the grave which Jesus in His humanity attained. This is, then, the way to look upon Easter-day, not as though Jesus Christ did something simply through His Divine nature, but to look upon Him as bearing testimony to our possibility.

Now, it is possible to carry this out in considerable detail, and to see how the idea especially represented in that resurrection of Christ was also the idea which is represented in the resurrection, or the power of resurrection in every human creature. Let me read to you again the deep words in which St. Paul has tried to crown the whole story of the power by which Jesus Christ arose. "In that He died, He died unto sin once; but in that He liveth, He liveth unto God." That text declares a perpetual fact concerning Jesus, and that perpetual fact is life. It is belonging to God which makes life the perpetual fact. Existence reaches back to an eternity past man's conceiving. It reaches forward to ages which never shall be finished. But there came into the long life of Jesus a certain experience, a certain episode and accident, we may almost say, in which He entered into the power of death. Then, as an event in His life, He did perish and die. But there was a life which He did not lay down underneath the life which He did lay down. The perpetual, uninterrupted fact was life. You see, then, what is the meaning of these words. They are a declaration of the continuous law of Jesus' life and of an especial event in Jesus' life. The special event does not interrupt or break the law. He was the ever-living one, even when He was hanging on the cross, and cried: "It is finished!" and gave up the ghost. Death came as an accident, through contact with our human sin. The everlasting life was of the nature of His being. "In that He died, He died unto sin once; but in that He liveth, He liveth unto God." Inasmuch as God is the perpetual element of the universe, and sin is an intrusion upon the universe, which shall pass away, Christ's connection with sin was a temporary thing, but Christ's connection with God is an everlasting thing. He died unto sin once in one critical and awful moment in His long career, but in that He liveth He liveth unto God in the outstretched being that covereth all the eternities.

How it sets before us that which was in the soul of Jesus all the time! We can see that in the deepest moments of His perishing He always felt His vitality underneath the perishing. He is living to-day in the ever-blooming being of His eternal existence, and He looks back and remembers that time when He died as the awful incident in that living career, but not as the beginning, and surely not as the end of His existence.

If we are able to transfer the Saviour's experience to our experience, great things become clear to us, my brethren. If we can take those words of St. Paul, "Christ is risen from the dead, and become the first fruits of them that slept," or the Saviour's own words, "Because I live, ye shall live also" —observe, if we can take all such words to ourselves, what a great thing it will be. I see a man die to-day. I stand by his bedside in the solemn chamber, I hear the dropping tears of his friends, the wailing and lamentation of those whose hearts are breaking and whose homes are becoming desolate and empty. I watch him, and at last he dies. What has happened in that man dying? That which I have seen is clear enough. The heart that has beaten on forty or fifty or sixty years like the pulse of a great engine which carries a big ship across the ocean, has stopped at last beside the wharf on the other side. The ship has come to the place it was sailing for all the while. That man has reached the climax of his earthly career. That man is dead. What is it that has come? A minute ago I was talking with him. He was speaking to me of the loves and dreams and imaginings with which I have been familiar, as I have known him these forty years. Now that is stopped. The man is dead. Shall I believe that an end has come to that vitality? The spiritual life is in the powers of the soul, not in the accident—shall I say?—which linked them in association with the body in which the physical change has taken place? Shall I believe that they have ceased, because it has ceased to be their minister? Shall I believe that the voice behind the trumpet is silenced for ever, because the trumpet has been broken to pieces? Shall I believe that the sun has ceased to shine in the heavens, because the sunlight has been broken and dimmed and clouded, and can no longer tell the story of the sun's power and spread his glory abroad upon the earth?

No, my friends. Death is simply something that happens to the bodily life. It remains altogether to be proved that death comes to that inner life, in which man's resolutions and thoughts and consecrations and lovings have been abiding always. Science speaks to us, and her declaration is more and more clearly this: "I have nothing to say in regard to the soul and its destinies. I have only to speak in regard to the body." Modern science —such is the latest utterance from many of her best voices to us—has nothing whatever to say which conflicts with or makes impossible man's continuance in human life as he passes forth into a different being, freed from that which was the instrument, but also the prison of the human soul.

Since we know that in Jesus continuance of being was an element which could not be broken, and upon the bosom of that element the special event of his dying rested as an incident and a phenomenon, but not as a destruction of the continuous power of life, shall we not believe that it is even so with man, whose life is linked with Jesus' life? For us, too, the great fact is a continuous existence, reaching how far back we cannot tell— reaching into what regions before we entered upon this special stage of existence we cannot begin to tell, but certainly reaching forward and continuing, now that it has begun. Into this existence there must come the incident of dying. The soul must look back from the midst of the endless ages and remember: "Once I died. Once death came to me in the course of this life which has stretched forward into the endless eternity. Once it came to me to die and I now remember it, as the ocean remembers the wave which was formed upon it, not as an interruption, but as a special expression of its life."

If this be so, then our human life which we are living to-day is a very great thing, if we are able to comprehend it. It is possible for us to make it very great, or make it very little. Do you not see how it is possible for me to live either in that power of continuous existence, or in the special incidents or accidents which form themselves upon it? Most men live almost altogether in the special incidents or accidents; the business which they do, the intercourse which they have with one another, the sicknesses through which they pass, and finally death. But these are only incidents upon the surface of our lives. Our life all the time is deep below, imperishable, and unchangeable. It is possible for a man to live underneath these incidents, to make the real thought of his life that which is continually inspiring and shaping all the real issues of his existence, the thought that he belongs to God. Men forget that and live merely in the power of their accidents and under the impulses of their perishable nature.

But there was a man who forgot the outward incidents of life, the perishable things, and lived in the inward fellowship of God. The life of Jesus Christ shows that it is possible for a man to live so that the base things of life shall not touch him.

How real to many of you seems the world about

you. How unreal that great word of God! You say in your creed, perhaps, that you believe in the reality of the heavenly things; but you say it, oh, how lightly! And another man declares his unbelief, and his unbelief is as flippant as your assertion is careless. But how deep it was to Christ! The outward things gathered their reality for Him only from the welling up within Him of the thoughts that were in the very life of God. Oh, so to feel our life and our doings in these lower ways as what they are that we may comprehend the profound life, the unchangeable life in which we are to abide forever and forever!

It is good to think of the eternal life as the Divine life. In that he liveth, he liveth unto God. It is not simply continuance of existence. The doctrine of Easter is not simply the notion that our human life is to last for ever and ever; that you and I are to go on doing these things that we are doing now through all eternity. How dreadful that would be! "I do not want to live for ever," says a man who is wearied with the monotony of life, as he looks forward with joy to the time when he can lay it down. You must get a deeper understanding of life before you can see immortality to be desirable or possible. On the other hand, you must get a sense of immortality before you can see the possible Divineness of your life. Life seems a noble thing to a man who can really comprehend them both. He will be so conscious of eternity that it shall seem to be unworthy of a soul that is going to live for ever to be busied with mere trifles. Oh, get deep—this is the lesson of Easter day—get deep into the things you do. Get into their fundamental principles and everlasting truths. Then you shall know yourselves to be immortal. On the other hand, knowing yourselves immortal by the revelation of Jesus Christ, you shall be forced into the very depths of these great things—great things which you are making little things, and in which you are living every day. For there is no great thing which may not be treated as a little thing and no little thing which has not a great and profound meaning if we will only find it.

I think if we sum up in one great word that which a continual sense of immortality would give to human life, we should take the word " nobility ". Do you not know that there is a certain sense of nobility which belongs to the greatest and finest things which men do ? There are poets and poems; but there are among the multitude of poems certain noble poems which evidently come from an exalted condition of the singer's emotions and which exalt him who reads them. There are pictures and pictures, some are fascinating and charming; but there are other pictures that are noble. There are actions that are charming, actions that make interesting changes in the outward world. But there are certain other actions which the instinct of man immediately designates and denominates as noble actions—actions which come from broad and rich and deep elements of human nature and which appeal to the noblest parts of the nature of those who see them. So there are men of all kinds, and among them stand forth certain noble men.

What are the qualities of this nobility? Certain things must be in them. The noble man, the noble poem, the noble picture, the noble deed has generosity in it. This of itself is simply part of some great system, living an individual life in that system, but finding its best service in doing the will of that system. It conceives of principles and not simply of methods. It looks abroad and does not confine itself to the present. The noble poem sings with a loftier strain, the noble picture portrays the diviner life, the noble deed sounds with the most thrilling power in human ears, the noble man takes possession of men, as no most fascinating creature to whom we cannot give the name really does.

Now, where shall that nobility come from? It is not altogether the bad men and bad women whom we meet, and the foul and deceitful things they do, that weigh upon us. We feel that these men and women who go crouching through their little ways were meant to stand upright and walk with firmer tread. We feel that a loftier spirit might be in all our human life, that there might be more nobility in humanity. Where shall it come from? Let every man and woman count himself immortal. Let him catch the revelation of Jesus in His resurrection. Let him say not merely, "Christ has risen," but "I shall rise. Not merely He underneath all death and change was unchangeable, but in me there is something that no stain of earth can tarnish and no stroke of the world can bruise. I, too, am part of God and have God's immortality in me." Then nobility must come. Until men's souls shall be full not merely of the knowledge, but of the genius and spirit of immortality, we shall be the ignoble things we are.

Lift yourselves up to-day. Know yourselves the children of God, immortal with the Father's immortality. And you will do the same things on Easter Monday that you did on Easter eve, but they will be done by a nobler being, and therefore they will be nobler things. Every day as you go on doing the same things they will become nobler things, as you grow into the sense of communion with Him whose immortality you share.

Oh, my friends, believe what we have said this morning, what all our service has said, what the event which we celebrate to-day says. In distress, in bereavement, oh! believe it. That death of your child three months, six months ago, some time since last Easter day, came as an incident of his life, and did not break his life, which is going on to-day. In that he died, he died unto sin once; but in that he liveth, he liveth unto the sinless

God. Your child, your friend, your brother, your sister, is living, and can never die.

You who are in doubt and in distress because of doubt, who say the creed with half faith, until by-and-bye you do not say it at all—not in uncertainty, but in certainty is the ultimate condition of the human soul. God will not let His children go in darkness and wandering always, He keeps the light and the truth as the real home of His children's souls. Be perfectly sure that if you keep your hearts entirely honest and true in the midst of doubt, the time will come when the truth will be absolutely clear to you, and you will look back and know that your doubt was an incident and an episode, while certainty is the continuous experience of life. In that you doubted, you doubted unto sin once, but in that you knew, you knew unto God.

And you who are living in sin learn that it is not necessary that sin should be perpetual; learn that it has but a weak hold upon your nature, because it is an intruder, a foreign thing that has no right there. Learn from Easter day that the deepest truth of life is holiness and not sin. Lift yourselves up, claim your heritage in God and Christ, drive out the tyrant, drive out the sin which has no business in your life.

Not our own sins only, but the great, flagrant sins of the world; this cruelty treading down the helpless under the heels of the powerful, this self-indulgence, this foulness, making a great mass of corruption out of what ought to be the garden of God—shall there not be something in Easter day that shall make us strong to fight it all—the certainty that not wickedness but goodness is what belongs in the world, that sin and death are an intrusion, and that light and law and holiness are the real possessors of this world!

THE ETERNAL LIFE.

"And this is life eternal, that they might know Thee, the only true God, and Jesus Christ Whom Thou hast sent."—St. John xvii. 3.

When Jesus said these words the transitoriness of life was pressing upon Him and His disciples. The words are part of the prayer which He prayed to His Father at the table of the Passover Supper. He had told His disciples that He was to leave them. All their life together was hurrying to its end. Have you never heard suddenly that some state of things which had lasted long, and been full of happiness, was to be broken up? And do you remember how everything belonging to it flashed into sudden brightness? The association, the sympathy, over which the knife was hanging, never seemed so dear; the comfortable surroundings had never seemed so necessary as now in the prophecy of their removal. A sickening, despairing sense of instability seemed to come over you and to cloud everything. *Nothing* seemed permanent or trustworthy. If you remember that you know how these disciples felt. Life had been shattered into dust, or melted into mist, for them by Jesus' words. And then, when life seemed frailest and most unreliable, they heard Him praying these very words to God: "*This is life eternal*".

The assertion of a sort of life, something in life, which lasted and did not go to pieces—the calm reminder that in the midst of all unstableness there was in man's thought and being that which could not perish, but must go on for ever, must have come in very solidly and nobly. So often, when we are most conscious of mortality, when disease is triumphing over that which disease can touch, when the ruins of what was fairest are all about our feet, a single word, the least reminder of that which is immortal, restores us, puts strength into our feeble knees again, and courage into our frightened hearts.

What is it, then, whose eternity Jesus proclaims so confidently? When everything else stops, what is it that goes on? When everything else decays, what is it that is imperishable? What is the core of permanence in this nebulous and shifting life? Jesus says it is the knowledge of God and of Himself—"*To know Thee, the only true God, and Jesus Christ Whom Thou hast sent*". Now, remember that the knowledge of God and of Jesus Christ must mean, and in the Bible always does mean, a personal relationship with God and Christ. It is not mere absolute knowledge. Man cannot know God absolutely, but only as God relates Himself to him. It is what He is *to us*, not what He is in Himself, that we may know of God. So that to know Christ and God is to have *to do* with Christ and God in the way of love and service. And Jesus says that the permanent part of our life—that which is eternal, that which must last, and cannot perish—is the part which has to do with God. Is not that His meaning?

Here is a very clear and simple test of all our life. Our houses must decay. What is there in them that will last? That which had to do with God. Not their bricks and mortar, but the tempers and the hearts that were cultivated in them. Our institutions will perish—even the systems of our Churches and the machineries of all our sacred things. But that which really knew God in them, the spiritual life which they enshrined no tooth of time can touch. Our friendships have a promise of permanence only as they are real spiritual intimacies knit in with one common union to God. The closest earthly ties, of husband and wife, of father and child—I know no reason to believe that they can outlast this natural state save as they themselves are more than natural, and bind the spirits to each other. Everywhere the body of things shall perish, and the soul, which alone knows and has conscious relations with God, lasts. Everywhere this is the only life eternal, *to know God*.

There is, then, something which is eternal if

men only knew it rightly; something which decay cannot touch; something which goes through death as the sun goes through a cloud and comes out clear upon the other side. When we fasten our thoughts on this, how it changes the whole aspect of the lives and deaths of men! Here is a poor holy man dying. How little difference death makes to him! How little change between the moment when he draws his last breath here and the moment when he breathes the new ether of the life beyond! Remember, he is to keep all that has to do with God and to lose all the rest. What is there for him to lose? His whole life has been lived with God. How much there is that he will keep! All his life is eternal. But another man, so much richer, lies dying in the next house at the same time. What an enormous change death is to him! All his life has been worldly. What is there that he can keep? How almost everything he must lose! How all that he has had seems to be mortal, grows colourless and threatens to die as he comes into the atmosphere of death! When we see how generally death seems to exchange the lots of men, making the rich seem poor and the poor seem rich, it makes the river that we all must cross seem like that stream in Greece of which the ancients told this fable, that it kindled every unlighted torch which was dipped into it, and quenched every torch which was already lighted.

We have seen, then, that there is a thread of

eternity running through human lives, something in all their transitoriness which must endure. A man may not know in his own life what it is. He may have no such spiritual perception as lets him accurately feel the difference of quality between an act of love and an act of selfishness. It may be that it is only in the loosing of the silver cord that its close-twined strands can be untwisted and distinguished from each other. It may be that the tares and wheat must grow together till the harvest before they can be separated; but none the less it is true that between the acts which you do runs this enormous difference; one is an act which shall be over for ever before the quick eye can fairly see that it is done; the other is an act which shall go on for ever, and be as much alive as now when eternity itself shall have grown old.

And this reminds us again of another truth, which we cannot be reminded of too often; or, rather, this is another way of stating the truth that eternity is not a mere privilege given to certain things and certain people. The eternal part of us is not that which God shall choose at some future day to endow with everlasting life. Eternity is a true quality in the thing itself. That which is to exist for ever has now in it the essence of its immortality. It is nobler now than the perishable thing beside it. It not merely is to be, it is eternal. The power of the endless life is the power of the present life. That part of us which is to outlive the grave, and to go on and on and on into a length of life where the imagination and the faith ache when they try to follow it, is to have that superior continuance only because it has *now* a superior nature, and is to be the permanent part of us because it is now the great and significant and important part of us.

There is always a tendency in religious thought, with its strong drawing towards the world to come, to throw itself forward into the future, to imagine conditions there which have no weight or reason in the present, and to speak as if that which is of subordinate and inferior importance now were by some change of circumstances to come out into supreme importance by-and-by. That cannot be so. *It is our relationship to God that is to make us live for ever, and that relationship must be at the bottom of our life now.* If our religion or connection with Him is to produce our future life, it ought to, it alone worthily can, shape our present life. That which is to run out longest must first be down deepest in us.

This really brings me to what I wanted to preach about to-day, although, letting myself be delayed by thoughts that came up by the way, I have been thus long in reaching it. *It is the regulative and shaping power of a Christian faith in this life.* I have tried to show you that what is to be eternal in the future must be deepest and strongest in the present. But so many men seem to think of religion as something that belongs to heaven. Some day, when we come there, it will be of all-importance to us whether we know God and Christ; but now it seems as if other knowledge were more immediately necessary, more absolutely indispensable. I wish that I could show such men what a principle of life the Christian faith is here and now; how it touches and transforms the obstacles which they meet every day; how it supplies exactly the deficiencies which they are recognising every day in their own lives. The Christian faith —by that I mean, remember, simply this: the strong desire to serve God, out of loving gratitude for the redemption by Christ.

Let me try to do this. I cannot tell you how earnestly I want to do it. I do not speak of the way in which the Christian faith arms a man in the few great, terrible temptations of his life. I do not speak of flagrant vices, of the power that Christ has to order a man's furious passions down. I speak of those constant deficiences of moral power which are recurring every day. They are what wear us out in time; they are the daily demoralisation of all of us. I appeal to your own consciences to recognise them as I speak, and then I beg you to see whether it would not lift a man out of all of them if he had the impulse of a redeemed soul serving God out of love; whether this would not be to him eternal life "*to know God and Jesus Christ Whom He has sent*".

What are the great deficiencies of daily moral life? *I mention first the difficult balance of responsibility.* Men know what duty is, but the balance, the even, steady pressure of duty upon the whole surface of a man's life is something which thoughtful men are always missing and wishing for in vain. The tendency of duty is to concentrate its strength in blows which strike with special and temporary force on some little spot of a man's life. On one day the sense of responsibility is overwhelming. The next day it is all gone. This thing or that thing I feel a tremendous compulsion driving me to do. There are other things (just as much my duty) I leave undone week after week without a pang. The consequence is doubly bad. Some tasks are wholly neglected, and others are done under a burden and a strain which exhaust us. Our life grows all spasmodic. Feverish, excited, anxious conscientiousness is constantly alternating with listless self-indulgence and indifference. We are driven all crazy with our work to-day, and to-morrow morning we are lying in the sun as if there were no work to do under the heavens. Do you not know that life? It is what Wordsworth describes in his great ode of "Duty":—

> "Me this unchartered freedom tires;
> I feel the weight of chance desires;
> My hopes no more must change their name;
> I long for a repose that ever is the same".

I know you understand it. I know that there

are thoughtful men and women here who would value it above every boon, who would be happy over it beyond all utterance, with a new sort of peaceful joy, if there could be given them to-day some power which, with broad, even weight, should press every duty into its place, crowding as steadily upon the little as upon the large, coming down from such a height above them that it should be independent of their whims and moods, and weigh upon to-morrow and to-day alike, not springing from themselves and so not changing with their changes, not fitful and feverish, but calm, serene, *eternal*. Is not that what we want? Give us that, and the "storm of life is passed," the haven of life is reached. We have entered on an unchanging and eternal life. Now hear our text again: "*This is life eternal, that they may know Thee, the only true God, and Jesus Christ Whom Thou hast sent*". O my dear friend, there is the answer to your longing! To love God out of gratitude, and to want to serve Him out of love—there is the rescue! The doing of all duty, not only for itself, but for His sake who wants it done, this is what puts force and pliability at once into duty, making it strong enough for the largest and supple enough for the smallest tasks, giving it that power which the great steam-engine has, with equal fidelity, to strike down a mountain and to pick up a pebble, adapting its movements to such different work.

When a man really enters into the Redemption of Christ, this one change takes place in him. Do not call it vague. Do not call it sentimental. It is intensely practical. It catches hold of the very heartstrings, and turns him to another life. This is the change. He does everything which he does, not because he wants to do it, nor because the world wants it, nor because it is abstractly right, but because His Master and Saviour wants him to do it. In that one change comes calmness into his life. So he attains the balance of responsibility. No duty is so heavy as to burden him, and none so light as to escape him. All are heavy and all are light at once for Christ—too heavy to be burdensome, too light to be contemptible. Is not that the redemption of responsibility?

Turn to another of the deficiencies which we all know—*the difficult sense of brotherhood.* We all know how hard it is to keep, not the conviction and the knowledge, but the certain feeling that all these men about us, out to the farthest end of the wide world, are our brothers, with a true cord of relationship between us and every one of them. I think that the decay of the power of feeling this is one of the sad things of all advancing life. It is not so hard for children. Youth has possible relations with all the universe. The young man has not settled yet into the fixed tastes and occupations which decide for him with whom he shall have to do. The most unlikely man that comes across his path may be the man who is to shape his destiny. And so he easily strikes hands with everybody, and has a certain superficial brotherhood with everyone he meets. But as the man grows older, his life draws in, grows sharp and definite and settled. The man decides just what he is going to be, and draws the outermost circle of all that he is likely to do in life. These definitions limit his intercourses and companionships, till by-and-by he has his little circle of associates, his family and business friends, to whom, if he is good-natured, he wishes well, but there is nothing more. He cannot reach out and take in a larger circle. Even patriotism is harder than it used to be. And to let his affection go sweeping out to the ends of the earth and down into the gutter where the outcasts lie—this seems preposterous, almost incredible. Ah! my dear friend, that is where you got the look of incredulity, the sceptical sneer, with which you are so ready now to greet as ridiculous any pretension that it is possible for a man to count his fellow-men his brethren and to care for them simply because they are the children of his Father.

But what then? How can one get this thought and distrust his limitations and in this large sense really grow humane? Ah! the thought is an eternal thought; the life which is lived in such a thought is an eternal life. And *"this is life eternal, to know Thee, O Father, God, and Jesus Christ Whom*

Thou hast sent". Surely that is plain enough. If I have lost sight of my brethren, I must go back to my Father to find them. It is in the Father's house that we must meet. It is possible for me to get a higher, broader thought of my life altogether. I am not merely getting a living among those who are in the same trade with myself, and therefore in some narrow sense are my brethren—not merely a merchant among the merchants, a lawyer among the lawyers, a minister among the ministers. These smaller fellowships break open when I am realising the redemption of Christ. I am a son of God, doing His will out of love; a son of God among the sons of God—that is, a man among men. This is the brotherhood into which we are redeemed. If you know God and Christ, you live in these deep relations, in this eternal life, and so you live with your brethren always. It shines in their faces on the street. It beats into music on the pavement as the tumult of their footsteps streams past your door. You are rescued by the Son of Man into the brotherhood of His brethren.

Then take another place in which the ordinary forces and supplies of life display their insufficiency. *I mean in the bearing of trouble.* Trouble comes to everybody, and what men ordinarily call the *bearing* of trouble is apt to be one of the dreariest and forlornest things conceivable. The tidings come to you that some neighbour of yours has felt the blow that sooner or later falls on every man. You go to him because it is your duty, wondering what you will find. You go reluctantly, fearing what you will find. Oh, how you hate and dread to go into that house of suffering, with its altered look, with the hush in its noisy entries and the darkness in its sunny rooms! What you do find is apt to be one or the other of two things—either a man all crushed and broken into fragments, with no strength, no courage, no manhood left; or else a man proud, cold, stern, hard, making believe that he does not feel, putting his sorrow away and trying to deceive you into thinking that he does not care. He does not succeed in deceiving you. Such "making believe" never really makes you believe. You pity him all the more for the wretchedness of his proud, hard misery. But now neither of these men is really bearing his sorrow, is he? Neither of them has really taken his trouble on his shoulders to carry it whither he pleases, taken it into his heart to give it his own colour and meaning. Each of them in different ways is borne by his sorrow. Their trouble has taken them upon its shoulders and is carrying them off into despair, has taken them into its cloud and is giving them its own gloominess. The man who is hardened by sorrow is as much the slave of sorrow as the man who is crushed by it.

And now, what is the matter with both these men? Simply that they laid out a plan of life which was not broad enough or deep enough to have any place for trouble. When they designed their lives they left sorrow out. A plan they had, a certain bright philosophy which answered well for the surface of things; but when the shock came, when the ground was opened and down below appear those deeper needs which lie underneath all these pleasant lives—when those needs lifted up their voices and cried, "Give us our satisfaction," these men had no answer to return. So many lives are like ships that sail to another land in the brilliant morning of a summer's day, and by-and-by, when they are out in mid-ocean, and the night comes, and the sky and water both grow black, find that they have brought no lights of any kind. They never thought of the nighttime when the morning shone so bright. And so these men never thought of the profound and the eternal when the superficial and the temporary looked so brilliant. And then, if I turn aside and find a man who really does bear his sorrow, who carries it, not jauntily as if it had no weight, but solidly and strongly as if the strength were equal to the weight, what is it that is different in him? It must be this: that he has some notion of life which is large enough to take in trouble. He has got some idea of a government of the world so wide that under its great laws some parts may well suffer for the blessing of the whole. He has got sight of an education of himself so deep and thorough that it cannot touch only the pleasant things of life. That great Fatherly Government is God. That deep Personal Education is Christ. The Christian enters into the profoundness of consolation because he loves his Governor and his Educator. "*This is life eternal, to know Thee, the only true God, and Jesus Christ.*" Oh, my dear friends, however bright the day be with you now! oh, young glad hearts in all the brilliant morning of existence! oh, ships that sail so gaily out to sea!—be sure you have the Light on board. Be sure of that, and then go on. Make life as happy as you will. See every hour shine with joyousness. When the darkness comes—as it will surely—the light is not far off. You need not go to seek it. You have it with you. The darker the night grows the brighter that light will shine. Only be sure you take it with you now. Be sure you take *it* — HIM — CHRIST — THE LIGHT OF LIFE.

I name only one more of the manifest deficiencies of human life; but it is one which presses upon us not occasionally, not merely in some special crisis. It is one whose presence we are always feeling. I know not what name to give it unless I call it *the lack of nobleness*. There come occasional, exceptional moments in every man's long life when, if only for a flash, he feels that he is living *nobly*. Something makes him forget himself, with ardent enthusiasm fire up for a principle, with reckless disregard of policy indignantly denounce a vice, with easy scorn push back temptation, with deep delight glory in some friend's greatness, greater than his own. The man is pitiable who has known no such moments. They stand up like peaks out of the fields of memory, and throw their light along the dead level of a life. Many a man is living now in the remembered radiance of some such long-gone day when he felt himself noble. But one or two such days in a man's life only show out by contrast the general low level at which our lives are lived. There is a littleness that wearies us. There is a drag to everything that makes us ask, "Is it worth while?" There seems to be an endless doing of details without any attainment of results, an endless laying of brick with no house getting built—a calculating, selfish, sordid life.

The elements of this vague spirit in life which we call nobleness seem to be chiefly these: The power of ideality, or the discerning of the ideas of things or people without being blinded by their circumstances; the power of enthusiasm, or intense hope; the power of devotion, or of forgetting one's self in a cause; and the power of indignation, which lifts one away from sin by contempt and hatred for it, not simply by fear of its consequences. A mean life, a low and sordid life, is low and sordid just because it lacks these powers. The man who cannot see through circumstances, who despairs, who is selfish, and who dreads not sin, but pain—he is your ignoble man, and it is the extent to which all these ignoble things are in all our lives that makes our ignobleness. But take a really noble life, and out of these elements there comes a certain exaltation into everything it says and does. It seems to walk on higher ground, to breathe loftier air. It lightens a room or another life when it comes into it. Paul was a noble man—idealist, enthusiast, devoted, indignant, a great lover and a great hater. And the life of Jesus crowns the summit of all human nobleness: insight, enthusiasm, devotion, indignation—He lived in these continually.

Have I not already suggested what I would say next? that all these qualities which make up nobleness must become permanent and constant in any man who really knows and loves God and Jesus Christ. Be a Christian constantly, and you must be noble constantly. Many have called themselves Christians and been the meanest among men; but none the less, all the more certainly, I say, BE A CHRISTIAN. Know Christ's redemption, and seeing all things redeemed in Him, their possibilities, their ideas, must shine out to you. Unite your life to God's, and it must glow with the enthusiasm of certain hopes. Give yourself up to your Redeemer, and you must be rescued from selfishness. Love God, and you must hate His enemies, treading sin under foot with all His contempt and indignation. Ah! with all the sordidness among us, there still are noble men and women in the world. Some of them are rich and some are poor. That makes no difference. They talk all languages. They wear all kinds of clothes. They hide their nobleness under various disguises, but it finds its way through them all. And the power of the nobleness in all of them—that which. makes them fine, pure, dignified, serene, eternal—is everywhere the same; the knowledge of God and Christ. The lofty life is that which, dedicated to the Saviour out of love, has been taken up with Him into heaven, and is hid with Christ in God.

Thus, then, I have passed through the ground which I proposed. See where our thought has led us. There are certain great defects in human life: the *lack of even responsibility;* the *lack of brotherhood;* the *lack of strength in trouble;* the *lack of nobleness.* Because of these great lacks, our life grows shallow, weak, and meagre. But, at the bottom of all these is a lack of profoundness, a defect of the serious and of the eternal in our lives. That comes to a man when, rescued by Christ from sin, he gives himself up to the Christ who has redeemed him. This is life eternal, to know Christ and God. Ah, it will not do to fling all the precious work of Christ off into an eternity unrealised and indistinct. *Now, here,* He saves us. This Christian man who even now does every duty for his Lord, and honours all his brethren, and takes the trouble that is sent him, and understands it and bears it, and is clothed with nobleness as the stars are clothed with light — is not that man *saved already?* Must he wait for the other side of the river before he reaches the fulfilment of the promise that "*he shall walk with Christ in white?*" No, indeed! "*Now* is the accepted time. *Now* is the day of salvation." Not far away, but *here* in your own homes, in your familiar works, wherever Christ can come, you can know Him, and enter into the eternal life by Him.

And yet, far away, too, there is something which there is not now to urge us on. This is the beginning, but there is much more before the end. The deeper we know God and Christ, the stronger and richer grows our eternal life. When we come to that heaven where the Lord God and the Lamb are the light and glory, then in perfect knowledge perfect life shall come. It begins here. Death has no power to intercept it for a second, and it goes on to completeness before the throne of God. May He grant it to us all!

THE RESCUE OF A SOUL.

"And He said, A certain man had two sons."—St. Luke xv. 11.

THE story of the Prodigal Son is the story of the real and the ideal in human life. They are identical with one another in the design of God. The life a man lives and the life he ought to live really belong together. Man has no right to live any other than the real and true life. The real and the ideal lie together in the thought of God. The parable represents the way in which the ideal goes forth to meet the man who has fallen into sin, and to lead him back from that which to him is actual. The prodigal has awakened to a sense of the ideal which has never perished. He desires to go back where the elder brother has been living under the father's smile and surrounded by the atmosphere of the father's love. Then comes the struggle to obtain the ideal. At last the ideal and the real shall be reconciled to one another. The real shall attain to the ideal and be brought back to that which at first it was designed to be. The whole of human life is embraced in that great story.

"*I will arise and go to my father.*" The instant

in which the boy perceives the wretchedness of his life the thought of his father's house arises. Think of him awakening to his wretchedness and having no father's house to go to! What shall we say? Suppose that man, having wandered from God, had no chance to return. Suppose, then, he did come to his sense of the misery and wickedness and dreadfulness of sin. Would it not be almost a curse that he should know his sinfulness if it was impossible for him to turn back to the God against Whom he had sinned and from Whom he had wandered? I think we cannot say that absolutely. I think we cannot say that it would be good for a man not to know his sin even if there were no chance for a rescue. Probably it would be better, because more truthful and honest, that a man, even though there were no hope for him, no Father to whom he could return, should still know the sin into which he had fallen and see the wretchedness of his life. There would be something like salvation even in that self-consciousness. But it would be a dreary salvation. It would be a dreadful picture that would be shown to us—this poor creature waiting in the outskirts of his Father's house and never able to come back to Him.

How different from that is the picture given to us here! It has all grown so familiar, we have become so used to thinking of hope as immediately associated with repentance, that we do not often think how dreadful repentance would be if there were no hope to which we could immediately turn. The picture becomes wonderfully clear to us. We realise it in the beautiful experiences of multitudes of souls. The picture of hopeless repentance does not come unless we seek after it; but when we do seek after it, how terrible it is!

Even before man repents God is summoning him. The soul in sin has the seeds of the salvation that shall come to him some day in the never lost sense that he belongs to God, in the welcome sounding to him out of his Father's house. We want to bring our souls to feel this. We want to come down to the very root of our lives in order to get rid of our frivolity and disobedience and to be led by the great hope which is open to us as the children of God. Let our effort be to realise ourselves in our sin; but let us be certain that we can realise ourselves in our sin only as we realise ourselves as the ideal children of God.

How is it in regard to the whole matter of the repentance of our sins? I am sure I speak the experience of very many of those who are listening to me, when I say that one of the hardest struggles of man is to realise his sin. I can see indications of sin in my soul; but to be conscious of my sin; to understand how wicked I am; so to feel my own wickedness that I can turn away from it— many a man will bear testimony with me that to do this is no easy thing. You take a paper and make a catalogue of your sins. Then you rise up and your conscience tells you that you are not so troubled with your sins as you ought to be. You do not hate them with all your soul. Again and again you go through the reiteration of this after cataloguing your sins. My friends, where is the difficulty? It seems to me just here: I shall never know how sinful I am by simply thinking over the sins that I have done. I can come to know that only by coming into some atmosphere where I may understand what God intended me to be. Only so can I confront my sinfulness as I want to and escape from it into the glory of the resurrection. Cataloguing sins may help us to this. Unless it does I think more and more that it has very little use and purpose. In itself the mere reckoning of wicked things done never can make a soul hate its wickedness.

If we think of sin as something which is going to receive vengeance by-and-by, it may make us tremble and shudder to think how the lash is to be laid upon the soul; but that is not a real repentance. Real repentance is only the soul's hatred for the absolute condition of wickedness because the soul desires and loves and longs for the condition of holiness.

Therefore the picture of the prodigal comes very close home to us. It was not the sense of the distinctive misery of his wretched life so much as the thought of what was waiting for him at home that made the prodigal say, "*I will arise and go to my father*". "*How many hired servants of my father have bread enough and to spare?*" That thought came down through all the stretch of distance which he had wandered, and it was the child's heart that was appealed to. The swine were contented, and knew no cause for grumbling; but to him, when the child's heart heard the father's appeal, that was the seed and source and fountain of his bitterness. As long as that memory came to him, it was impossible for him to be satisfied to remain where he was. It was the appeal of the father's love for him that loosened him from the low associations which his outward life had lived, and made ready to go back into that home which had been waiting for him all the while. It is the thing we may be that creates discontent with the thing we are.

That thought is set forth in the great truth of our Christianity, the truth of the Incarnation. Christ is the ideal humanity, coming out to seek the real humanity. The statement that God made man in His own image seems to me the Old Testament correspondent of that which is declared in the New Testament—"*A certain man had two sons*". The real humanity, paralysed and broken down, is only too ready to become contented with wretchedness of living. Then comes forth the ideal humanity, then comes Jesus in His Incarnation. He came unto His own, and His own received Him not. "*To His own.*" He came to those who had sonship to God as He had. He came unto them and they received Him not. "*But to as many as did receive Him He gave the power to become sons of God.*" The Incarnation is the story of the prodigal son told in the glorious history of Jesus Christ, who came forth from the Father and came into the world. If, then, you would realise the story of the prodigal son in yourselves, you have to listen to the voice that comes out of the warm heart of God and calls you back again to Him; and that voice is Jesus Christ. Do you not see how this story in our own day is the story of the rescue of a soul by Jesus Christ?

That is a beautiful conclusion: "*I will go to my father and say, I have sinned against heaven and before thee, and am no more worthy to be called thy son; make me as one of thy hired servants*". He felt that he had no right to occupy a son's place. If there was a new life for him in the father's house it should be lived among menials; and yet, even while he says that, while he accepts that as the only possible place, at the bottom his soul is conscious that it cannot be so. Even as he goes to present himself and calls, "*Father, make me as one of thy hired servants,*" the old name clings upon his lips and the old consciousness is still in his soul. Shall we say there was falsehood and affectation in this pretence of his that he thought himself only worthy to occupy a menial's place? Not so. He thought himself unfit to be a son, and yet he had such insight into the father's love that he knew his father could only receive him as a son. That is the true position of the sinner as he comes back to his Father. He knows he has forfeited everything, yet he knows that everything is his. He goes up to the Father saying: " Let me do the lowest and most drudging work ". Yet he has such a perception of God that when the Father receives him and pours upon him the bounteous hospitalities of His love it does not seem strange to him. He enters into it and takes possession of it with all his humility still preserved, yet he knows he has a right there as His Father's son.

That feeling is in some of your hearts, I hope, this morning, as you are turning back to God. May I not trust that some soul here has really caught sight of the tremendous difference between the life it has been living and the life it might live? If that soul really is in earnest there is a consciousness of two things in that soul. One is the consciousness of how far off that life is from God, and the other is the consciousness of how near it is. And the two together make the soul's salvation. If it did not seem so far away the soul would think it easy to do that which it is a great and profound thing to do. On the other hand, without the second consciousness there would come despair. Know the difficulty of salvation. Know the easiness of salvation. Know how far from God you are. Know how near to God you are. Keep all the fear of the Christian life. Keep all the hope of the Christian life. Struggle as if God was so far off that you would need all your strength to come to Him. Leap as if one single bound could carry you out of your wickedness into His righteousness and love.

"*Father, I have sinned against heaven and before Thee.*" There are two specifications. Heaven is the everlasting righteousness, the great body of Divine law. Therefore, the conscience, feeling essential and intrinsic guilt, recognising the sin against the Divine order, says, "*I have sinned against heaven*". But the Father is the perfect personal love. To sin against Him is not merely to break the law, but it is to wound the affection of the Father in His love towards the child. So the child in our earthly household may come to the father and say, "I have done wrong, my father, and I have given you pain". The child, remorseful and yet hopeful, stands before the father and makes confession of sin. My friends, we know in our consciences that we have sinned against eternal law and done our little part to break the perfect order of the universe. Our soul knows that the heart of our Father is pained. Sometimes conscience, and then again sometimes the soul, only repents. When conscience and soul, when the total man repents, then the whole nature of God is taken hold of.

You know what a difficulty there is among theologians with regard to the ability of man to come to God. It does seem to me that the parable of the Prodigal Son makes it clear. There is no ability in man except the Father draw him. There is no ability even to draw him to the Father except as the Father enters in and takes possession of the soul within the child. The soul is among the swine until the Father's love comes and seeks him. But the Father's love does come and seek him. Let there be no question in your souls of your ability. We can, not because there is power in this humanity of ours, but because this humanity of ours has been sought by the eternal love of God. And I know that Christ is seeking me to strengthen me, and I never need do another sin until I die. Multitudes I shall do. Again and again I shall break the law of Him whom I love, and whose law I fain would keep. But I need not do it. There is in that new unit made by the combination of His grace with my will the Power of absolute righteousness. It is only because I break that unit into its diversity again that I choose to sin, if sin shall stain my life through the remaining years. Let us know that ability comes by the entrance of Christ's grace into our lives—ability not our own, but brought to us by the grace of Him who redeemed us. Let the knowledge of that ability make us strong.

So let us meet our own particular lust or passion when, with its familiar audacity, it comes and says,

"My servant, do my will". Then we may say humbly, "By the grace of God, I am no servant of yours. I am the servant of Him to whom my soul rightfully belongs. Get thee behind me, Satan. Father, take me closer to Thyself."

Some of you are asking what repentance means. That is what it means, the soul ever saying to itself: "*I will go to my Father*". I hear one great host, all saying together "*I will go to my Father*". They are saying this with various degrees of perception of what that Father is and where. Some are saying it more intensely and some with less eager desire. But wherever men have tried to do right and escape doing wrong, have felt the ideal in life summoning them away from the actual condition in which they are living, there has been this great outcome of the human soul: "I will go, I must go to my Father; for there only can my soul be satisfied".

"LIKE AS A FATHER."

Psalm ciii. 13.

The verse that I would like to ask you to think about a little to-night is, it seems to me, the very verse we need for our Sunday evening worship here, and the very verse that a great many of us may need to carry away. I would ask your attention to the thirteenth verse of the hundred and third Psalm:—"Like as a father pitieth his children, even so the Lord pitieth them that fear Him". My friends, there are a multitude of persons in this world to whom those words have become precious; that is the simple reason why we have come here to-night. I remember a story in an old book. It says that in the old city of Babylon —and it must have been when the medical profession was in a far less advanced state than now —every man, when his friend was sick, carried him outside of the city walls and sat him just outside of the gate of the great city, and asked every person who passed by to give his prescription, to tell the best cure that he knew of for the disease. There must have been some strange prescription given, but the words of the story always attracted me. It is said that no man was ever so bad as not to tell the best he knew. Every man told what seemed to him best for the cure of the disease. Coming a little nearer, I think we can remember —those of us who are old enough to remember the stirring events of the past twenty-five years—that in the days during the war, when some great news came from the field of battle, some news that stirred the souls of the people to their very depths, and rejoiced their hearts at the prospect of the speedy termination of the war and the restoration of the Union, men went from man to man among those whom they met in the streets, not even questioning the source from which the information came: "Have you heard the great and glorious news? Do you know that the cause of the Union is sure to triumph?" We read that in the cities of Russia, at the beginning of every Easter Day, when the sun is just rising, men and women go about the streets greeting each other with the information, "Christ is risen". Every man knows it. But all these are illustrations of how a man, when his heart is full of a thing, wants to tell it to his brethren. He does not care if the brother knows it already. He goes and tells it to him again. And so, when the truth of Christ's Gospel shall come so home to each and every one of us that all men shall be filled with the glad intelligence and tell the story of how men are living in the freedom of their heavenly Father, it shall not be needful to have a revival of religion. Let us anticipate that time to-night, and on the two following Sunday nights. Let us go about telling each other that which we do believe thoroughly. It seems to me to be all crowded together, in those words of David: "Like as a father pitieth his children, even so the Lord pitieth them that fear Him".

I cannot forget the associations of this venerable hall, and the way in which, in the old days, men have stood here who have been great among the orators of the country, and have addressed their fellow-citizens, and, stretching abroad their arms, have said, "Fellow-citizens," and then told them what they had to declare. I look around upon you, and I can address you to-night by a title far nobler than fellow-citizens. You are fellow-men and fellow-women. You have a common Creator with me, and, therefore, I dare to address you to-night as fellow-children of Almighty God. I want to speak to you to-night in these few words as if brother was speaking to brother, as man speaking to man, with the consciousness that we are all children of a common Father. For everything in religion finally comes home to that, that God is the head of the great house in which we are living. David had that in mind when he wrote this very psalm.

All through the Bible we find evidences of the relationship which God sustains to all of us. Men ransack the Bible for texts that can best bear out their dogmas and beliefs. He is called throughout the Bible by different names; sometimes He is called Lord, sometimes King, and sometimes He is called Master, and all of these are great words, and have great meaning; but, when the Bible tries to get hold of the best and richest word by which to describe God in His relationship to humankind, it speaks of Him as Father; and that definition, to my mind, goes before any other. It seems to me one of the reasons why the Christian religion has spread so marvellously throughout the world and over the earth is that it presents the relationship in which God stands to His people as that of a father to his children. There is no land in all the world where that relationship does not exist, and is not recognised as the most sacred relationship that can exist between two human creatures. You may travel down to the South, and, under the burning sun of the tropics, you find a father's love. You may travel up to the North Pole, and there you find it; and just so far as and wherever population reaches, you find a father's love, and precisely the same thing. Everywhere throughout the world there is this great common sign of humanity. There is a common language in which the human soul ever speaks and declares that the sacredest relationship is fatherhood, that relationship which a father holds to his child. Just see what that relationship means. That dependence means one life being backed by another life, and quite indiscriminate and indifferent to the moral condition of the one whom he loves. That seems to be the idea. Do you love your bad children worse or less than you love your good children? Do you love them with a different sort of love? No, you do not, but very often it seems as if a father or mother yearned toward the one that is most rebellious and profligate. When fatherhood is spoken of, it means that this love takes no notice of what the child has done or is in his character, but simply loves because he has been cradled in his arms in infancy, and remembers all the hopes and inspirations that have gathered round that child's love. It seems to me to mean so much when it says that God is the Father, and that is what it means. Underneath His approbation or disapprobation, underneath His approval or disapproval, there is great patience, indestructible love for us, because we are His children, whether the best or the worst of us; those who are living the most upright lives as well as those the most profligate are all Christ's children. You will remember the parable of the prodigal son, which I have just read, going and leaving his father's care, and outraging his father's love, and yet that father's love was so indestructible that he was ready to receive him home. You may go into the most horrible places that this city can show, and you cannot outgrow or leave it. His love pursues you. And that is the thing that is going to bring you back, if you are ever going to be brought back. So God calls Himself by that great name of Father, and puts His life behind every other life, and would give it something of the opportunity that belongs to the children. Look at the children playing in the street—look at them, with their easy and careless faces. What does it mean? It means that a father's love stands behind them; and something like that may come into our souls.

Now, I don't believe that a soul ever goes through life without resenting, at some time or other, pity. You may say, "Give me what help you may, but, above all things, don't pity me". When a man is down, and he sees friends come about him with their lips open, he wonders what they are going to say, and he feels like picking himself together and saying, "Don't pity me, whatever you do". Men scorn pity because pity is so apt to be scornful. Pity is a sort of mirror into which we look, and then it is a feeling that we all resent, partly because it is so useless to us, and partly because we hear people who say, "I pity you," and then leave us in the gutter because their pity does not go forth into action. No man resents pity as pity. At any rate, there are multitudes of people who resent the pity of their fellow-men. We say that God had pity. The child never resented the pity of its father. It is the intertwining of the lives that makes pity.

The child comes to the father and says, "Father, pity me". David says that is just like the pity of God. God pities you with a pity that has no particle of scorn in it. Many and many a man, who has resented the pity of his fellow-men, who has said to them, "I will not be pitied by you," has gone into his closet and said, "O God, pity me! I will not accept any pity except Thine, for Thy pity is full of love, and full of understanding, and full of the wish to help; and, O God, pity me with that love and pity which shall be the salvation of my soul!" You know it in your own soul, you know it in your own family, you know it among your children. You take pity on them. The father has the right to give pity when it will be taken from nobody else, and when nobody else has the right to give it. Yet I almost hesitate to ask them to tell their notions with regard to God from the way in which their own families are living. Do they really want me to talk to them in this way? Do they really want me to have them understand that God is to them just what they are to their children? Do they want me to go to them and say: "You ought to be to your children just what God is to you"? Where is the father that is willing to have his children draw their idea of God from their knowledge and experience of him? Here is a poor little child lying on his death-bed. He has lived the hardest sort of a life. His father and mother had beaten and abused him, and there was the entire absence of that fatherly feeling that is spoken of. The doctor comes to him and says, "My child, you are going to die". The child says, "What does that mean?" The doctor says, "You are going to heaven". The child looks in the doctor's face and says, "Will God beat me?" Was there ever anything more pathetic than that? "Will God beat me?" That was the only thing he knew of going to anybody. His life had been so absolutely wretched that he could not form any other idea. He had been so beaten that he could not conceive of any life to which he might look where he would not be beaten. There our parable fails, and it is impossible to picture out the condition of such a life. My friends, if your children are ever going to understand God, or to understand that great and helping love that lies all around us, and its encouragement and purport, the first picture of it must be in your own house and in your own life. Picture fatherhood to your own children in such a way that, when told that God is their Father, they don't shudder and hold back. Be to your children such a father that, when you say to them, God is, in His perfection, such a Father, they shall rejoice in and welcome and ask to see that Father who shall fully and completely express to them that which their earthly father demonstrated to them in their homes, and tried to express to them with his poor human life.

Then we have this picture, which we want to get deep into our souls—a jewel lies about the street, knocked and kicked about everywhere; men don't wear it about their necks until by and by, till at last it is set in some precious setting. When a man puts himself into the setting of the pity of God, then it is that the jewel of his life is placed in the setting that brings forth all its richness. A sword is not really a weapon, but is an absolutely useless thing till a hero takes it in his hand and goes forth to battle. When a man puts himself into the love of God he takes that life and says, O God, receive it and use it. Then it is like a dagger or a sword, because it is put into the hands of a great soldier. Then it is like a dagger knowing its own uselessness until it is put into the hand of a man who can use it, to do strong battle with and conquer with it. Such is the life of a man who has put himself into the very grasp of the love of God. It seems to me that there are three things that God pities in a human creature. That means you and me and every one of us. It belongs to every soul, every man and woman here. The first thing that he pities you and me for is that we fall so far short of what He meant us to be. You don't pity any star that shines with all the brilliancy it was intended to shine with. You do not pity any flower that puts forth all the brilliancy of colour which that particular kind was meant to have. But everything that falls short of its full and true life you pity. You pity the stunted tree. You who have lived in tropical regions and southern climates, and have seen the palm tree in all its majesty, and then have gone into the northern climate and seen its stunted growth, you pity that tree and wish with all your hearts that you could take it and put it into the other climate, in the region where it belongs, where it could get the sunshine it hungers for, where it could get the warmth it was made for. I don't pity the man who lives through all his life to an old age, and is surrounded with the respect of all his fellow citizens, and at last lies down and dies. I have no pity for that man. But the boy who dies with his powers just putting themselves out, who lies down and his vital spark is drawn from him, I cannot help feeling some sort of pity for. That life has not fulfilled its destiny. If every man lived out the fulness of his life, I don't think there would be anything like pity in the heart of God, but when God looks and sees that every man who lives falls far short of His ideal that every man was meant to be, then the heart of God Almighty goes out in pity for that life.

What glimpses we get of the greatness that is in us that does not come into action! Are you not amazed, not by seeing how few great men there are, but how many of them? I wonder at the heroism that is so common. People say that heroes are very rare. I think that heroes are plentiful. At least, that there are heroic moments in the lives of every one of us. Do you read the papers? You never see an account of an accident or calamity that you do not hear of some man who behaves like a hero, who, if he were only one man, would sit upon a pedestal where his daring must come to the attention of everybody. Where is the burning house in which a child cries out in agony that some one does not rush through the flame and rescue and save the precious life? Where is the crashing train that is going into impending ruin on some dark and tempestuous night, with precious souls on board, that the engineer, standing at his post, does not reach down, catch hold of the handle, and grasp it unto the very death? I tell you heroes are not so rare. Who doubts that, if the trumpet of war should blow again over our country, as it has been heard before, that the heroes are as plentiful to-day as they were in those days when the boys out of the school craved for a sword, and demanded the right to go forth and fight for their country? Who can stand still in this hall, this cradle of liberty, and think of the men who laid their lives down, at the very beginning of the government, for the very liberty we are enjoying to-day? Who can refrain from honouring the heroism that dared speak even in behalf of the oppressed and degraded? Yes; heroism is common enough. But the awful thing is this—that a man will fall back from the moment of his heroism, and do some mean, wretched, and degrading thing; do something that, if it were publicly known, would mark him as a poor craven, a hypocrite, and a coward. I am struck by this, and I am sure that you must have been at the way in which men think of their common life, and are not willing to think of the grand moments of their lives. Let me dare to remember, let you dare to remember, that some day you did a great heroic thing. A man meets you and says: "Are you the man that did that?" "Yes, sir." You have to tell the story. What does that mean? And you say: "Oh! that was the exception; that was the bursting forth of a volcano, the flash of a comet across my sky. This is my real life." Now, there is the blunder. The noblest thing you ever did, the noblest emotion you ever felt, the deepest, tenderest, most self-sacrificing act of your life—that is your true self, and not the baser life into which you have fallen.

How do we know that? Through Jesus Christ, who lived upon this earth a man. He had my humanity and yours in Him. He showed us what man was, as the full palm tree in the tropics shows what the real one should be when compared with the stunted one that you find in your conservatories. When I want to know what a man is, where shall I go? Shall I go to you with your cramped life, or shall I go to myself with all the base passions that I know are in me? No, I will go to Jesus Christ, the man who walked through human life and did everything that was appointed for H:m to do without a single flaw or failure; and in Him I see a man who opened His arms, stretched out His hands, and said, You ought to be men, just like Me, and He said, I go to My Father. He abides in Me, and I in Him. What did He mean by that? Do you ever read the Gospel so that you see the Lord Jesus Christ there? I think that people read their Bibles in such a stupid way that they cannot see Jesus Christ there.

From the midst of the New Testament pages there should stand out a man who should be for us a very pattern, a man Divine in all perfection. Have you ever seen Christ in those pages? If you have not, you have not read your Bible, you have not read the New Testament aright. If you had, you would have seen Him who walked about among men as if He walked about among the stars. He saw the best in every one of them and they revealed themselves to Him. Do you suppose that John and Peter were different sort of men from the men we have to-day? No. But Jesus saw the richness in them. Jesus saw that John and Peter and Andrew and all the rest of them were capable of leading Divine lives, so He beckoned to them, and He said, "Follow Me," and they followed Him, and great deeds followed them, and the divinity came out in them, and they shine in the great Gospel history like stars in the firmament. Jesus walked through the streets of Jerusalem and saw the children. He looked beneath the dirt, the selfish passions, and the sins and saw the image of their Father implanted upon their faces. Do you think it was so in the streets of Jerusalem only, one of the most wicked places in the whole world? Do you think that Jesus Christ does not go through the streets of Boston and see behind the vilest, the most dissipated, the most brutalised, the greatest reprobate, the image of His Heavenly Father? And what He is trying to do is to make these people feel just as He feels; not to put into them something that is not there, but to call out that which is in them.

Men are preached to that they are more wicked than they are—that they must not set so high worth upon humanity. I tell you we want another kind of preaching along with that. There is in every man something greater than he has begun to dream of. Men are nobler than they think themselves. When a man gives himself in consecration to Jesus Christ, then the nobility comes forth until he shines like a star. Go home and believe in yourself more. Go home and break the crust of your despair. Go home and ask Christ to let you see yourself as He sees you, all stained with sin, but the Divine in you all the time. I remember of saying once that when the pilgrims were baptised in Jordan that they might put away their sins, each one wore a pure white robe, and after he came out of the water the robe was kept until his burial day, and when at last he died he was buried in that robe. Then he came to his judgment-day, and when he wore that robe he was baptised in in the Jordan, he recognised it, and in his coffin he bore testimony to the life he had been living, and came back to the judgment of his own ideal. If you are cowardly, impure, and deceitful, God pities you; God pities you because you have fallen so far short of that which He meant you to be, and which He has never forgotten. It seems to me that God pities men for their sorrows and troubles. Oh! sometimes we say that God knows and He does not really pity us, for He sees to the end, and understands that our troubles are to be the means of our grace, so He doesn't pity us. And sometimes God comes to see that if He trains His children without a single pang, it would not be well. You see that your children have to suffer, but do you pity them any the less? Jesus knows what it is to suffer. The Man of men was the Man of sorrows too. There is no suffering that you have, whether men see it or not, whether men are smiting or not, but I see Him standing up among the poor people pitying them with all His soul. I see Him halt and hesitate, and pain comes into His face as He meets the funeral procession. I see Him by the thief on the other cross and pitying him with all His soul.

Is there no hope for you, O my brother, sister, in the knowledge that there is in the heart of God an ache because of that ache of yours; that Christ pities you; that God pities you for your suffering? No matter that He does see that by patient bearing of that pain, by the heroic confidence that comes of trust in Him He knows that some day you may tread it under foot, He pities you all the same. Infinite love can never exhaust it. Man is carried through life, through such valleys and over such mountains of suffering, until at last his strength is exhausted by his suffering, and God takes him into the home where there shall be no more suffering. He will be helped through his suffering and pitied by One who has a right to pity—One who knows what suffering is. He pities us most of all because of our actual positive sin. And human misery does not come to its culmination until man sins. A man comes to me and says: "I am in the deepest of pain. No man can be more miserable than I am." I say to him: "My friend, have you got yourself to blame for it? Have you done wrong? Have you sinned?" He says: "No, no; I am not to blame. I have not done wrong. It has come to me without any fault of mine." Then I say to him: "You are not the most miserable man on the face of the earth; you have not begun to touch the real depth of misery until self-reproach comes in and takes possession of your life". So God has infinite pity for the soul that has sinned. Just think of it. Here is a man standing by the window of some house. He sees a sick man go by, carried to the doctor's by some father or parent. He sees a staggering man go by with a crippled limb that is going to be his all his life, and he says: "Poor man!" He sees a poor, bowed form of a discouraged man, a man who has nothing the matter with his body, a man with no special pains, but whose life has been beaten down. Does he pity that man? That man knows himself to be a disgraced man. He knows that on his soul there lies guilt which is going to make him disgraced, and he envies those who go by with simple miseries. Simple misery is nothing compared with sin to make a man miserable.

Look at Jesus standing before Pilate. Did Pilate pity Jesus? Did Jesus pity Pilate? Yes, with all His heart, because He saw in Pilate that meanness that makes earth miserable. Look at the slave beaten by his master, and then read the pages of *Uncle Tom's Cabin*. While he was being beaten by his master, the slave cried out for pity, but really was pitying the master all the time. See the martyr burnt at the stake. Is it the executioner who has pity, or the martyr who pities the other? Ah! I think the way God escapes from hating His wicked children is that He pities them so that He cannot hate them. His own soul is filled with love. Nothing can be really successful and help forward except justice and truth be carried into all our relationship with one another. I must be a true, brave, just man before I can hope to be a happy one, and the community has got to have justice and righteousness in its heart before it can be the happy community for which we wish. We look forward to the changes that are coming, and we see them in the distance, and the good of those changes can only come when those who seek them are consecrated to justice and righteousness, and in seeking them will do injustice to no man.

There are three things for which God pities man. First, because he has failed in so much; second, because he has so much of wretchedness and sickness and misery; third, because he is a sinner. David says: "Like as a father pitieth his children, so the Lord pitieth them that fear Him". Does he mean God only pities good people? Surely not. God pities everybody. How will it be when the sun rises on our city tomorrow? When in the East, will it get into the windows of every house in this town? No, but every window that is turned toward the East, so that the sun shall have nothing to hinder it, every window that has invited the sunlight and is open to receive it, that sunlight shall come in without a doubt. Will Christ help every soul of you?

Will He redeem you all and help you out of sin? He will if you give yourself to Him, but He cannot if you do not give yourself to Him. It seems to me that every soul cannot fail to understand this. I talk about the movements of the planets, and I know that I am talking in a poor and in an imperfect language; but I say God loves me, and I know that is true. I say Christ saves me if I will be saved, and that is the one thing that I am absolutely sure of if I go back to Him like that prodigal son to his father, repentant. Man bows down in penitence and says: "O Christ, forgive me," and prays that prayer that millions have prayed—and would to God that some of you may go home and pray to-night to God for forgiveness, and say: "I will not leave until Thou hast forgiven me and taken my sins away." Then that becomes a very temple for God to enter into, and, lo! God comes and glorifies all his life. You cannot begin to imagine the magnificence of the human soul. The soul never begins to know its greatness until Christ comes in and claims it for His own, fills it with high desires, and makes it the temple of the Holy Ghost. He will do that for the souls of every one of you if you will let Him. There is nothing in the world for you to do except praying and letting go of the sins to which you have been clinging, and praying God to enter into your life.

CRYING AFTER CHRIST.

"*The Canaanitish Woman.*"—MATTHEW xv. 21-28.

THIS is one of the conversations of Jesus which, I think, derives a peculiar interest from the character and situation of the person with whom the conversation was held. Jesus generally confined Himself to the land in which the chosen people were settled. Galilee and Judea were the scene of most of His miracles and teaching. But once or twice He went across the border into that region near Jerusalem which never had been really conquered, but had always remained in the possession of the Canaanites and their descendants. It was on such an occasion that He met the woman with whom this conversation took place. She, in a general way, represented that great mass of mankind which lay outside the Jewish nation.

We often wonder how it was possible for Jesus, with all the great thought of humanity in His soul, to confine Himself to the little country of the Jews, to a people who were certainly not the most promising of the human race, yet to whom almost all His teachings were given and His mighty works shown. It seems to me that the position in which Jesus constantly worked is not unlike that in which a great many of us are compelled to work. We find ourselves living our life and doing our work in the midst of a little set of people and a various round of circumstances. Yet there are always pressing upon us the great multitudes of interests that lie outside, and we grow dissatisfied with life.

As nearly as it was possible for dissatisfaction to enter into the soul of Jesus, there must have been in Him something of the same feeling. How did Jesus meet that feeling? Surely He must have been able to see in them, as sometimes we, too, in our better moments, see in the few people who come within our touch, how representative they were of the great human race. He must have been able to realise that in them He touched the humanity which, separated as widely as it may be, is still one humanity from end to end. He knew that if His Spirit could go abroad and reach the furthest ends of the earth He would find still the same humanity with which He was dealing there; so that He did touch, and knew that He was touching, the great human race.

Then I think there is the great thought of the patience of Jesus Christ. He was the Lord of eternity. The few years He was living here upon earth were but an episode in His eternal service to the souls of men. He looked forward to the centuries and centuries which should pass after He had gone away from the sight of men, and knew that still He would be labouring for the souls of men. So He was infinitely patient. He knew there was time enough in His eternal life for the work which had been given Him to do. When these two great convictions come to us that were in the soul of Jesus; when we know that, touch human life as we may, we are touching the whole of it, and that no man can do any good work for his brother in any little region of the world and the most foreign and distant region of the world not be the better for it, and when we come to have something of the patience of Jesus, knowing that long after our work is past away His work will be going on, and we shall work in Him, then we shall work as Jesus worked. There comes contentment in the limited lot of life. If it ever oppresses and torments us that our lives are shut in, that there is so much work to do that we cannot touch, let us remember how the Divine Master lived those precious years of His life within the narrow walls of Judaism, and hardly laid His finger upon the multitudes of humanity lying outside, always present to His vision, yet shut out from the immediate work which He had come to do.

Yet it is interesting to notice how Christ did sometimes cross the border. It gives us some valuable suggestions. One of them, I think, is here. We can well believe that one who has been dealing with a nation which had received a peculiar preparation for His teachings would find a certain kind of freshness when He went abroad and encountered those who required the reiteration of first principles. It was as it is now, when one goes from preaching in our Christian America and begins preaching to the heathen nations who have never heard anything of Christianity. I can well believe that one would find a certain return to the first questions which spring out of the real depth of the human mind, and which do not belong to the more superficial conceptions, if he went and preached to the heathen and came in contact with fundamental and primeval humanity.

I think we can see something of that kind in the fifteenth chapter of Matthew. There are two parts to that chapter. In the earlier part Jesus is speaking to the Pharisees. They have a miserable little question about washing the hands before eating meat. They said to Jesus, "Your disciples are not orthodox. Look at them! They have not washed." Jesus had to tell the Pharisees that they themselves had made the commandments of God of none effect by their traditions.

Then, after this dispute, which I think must have been wearisome to Jesus, He crosses the border and encounters a simple human nature. A woman cries after Him with the cry of necessity. It is not something wrought out in the elaboration of ecclesiastical instruction, which demanded this and that arbitrary thing of His disciples. It is the cry that comes forever from the bottom of the human heart. This cry it was that came to Jesus when He went into the coasts of Tyre and Sidon. There is a certain sort of wildness, freshness, primariness about the cry of this woman. There was something deeper there than any question about washing hands before meat. Jesus is put to the test, not as to whether he would confirm the traditions and conditions of a single system, but whether He would meet the everlasting wants of human nature. There was the test by which He must ultimately claim and possess the world.

There are two sorts of Christian evidence. They are both true; but one is so much greater than the other. Sometimes we are pointed to the Old Testament, and told of certain prophecies which Christ fulfilled. We are pointed to a certain verse in Isaiah and another certain verse in Matthew; and we are told how one fulfils the other. We are bidden to observe how the whole system of prophecy in the Old Testament and the fulfilment in the New Testament correspond, part to part. There is an evidence of Christianity there; but it is not the great evidence. The human soul learns to believe in Jesus because of the way in which His presence comes to the immediate needs of the human soul. I believe in Jesus because He fulfilled the prophecy of Isaiah; I believe in Jesus so much more because He fulfils the prophecies in my soul. Andrew, when he had come to believe in Jesus, went and found Peter, and said: "We have found Him of whom Moses and the prophets did speak". And by-and-by another disciple finds Nathanael and tells Him that One has come who fulfils the prophecies of the Old Testament. It was a noble matching of the whole history of their race, with its anticipations and types, with that which had actually come among them. But how different from all this was the cry of the poor woman! "O Lord, thou son of David, have mercy on my daughter. She is grievously sick of a devil." These two evidences must be always in our hearts when we are trying to identify and believe in the Saviour. There must be a grasp upon that system which, reaching from the prophecy at the gates of Eden, fulfilled itself by-and-by when the seed of the woman set its heel upon the serpent's head. But there must be, underneath all that, this present sense of the way in which the love and hope and inspiration and salvation of Jesus satisfy the human soul.

So it was that this woman came to Jesus, with this wild fresh cry, out of suffering humanity. We should have said, from what we know of Jesus, that He would immediately give the desired help. But it is not so. There comes a reluctance, and that is what I want you to think about a while.

It has two parts. In the first place, there is the remonstrance of the disciples. And think how it was typical of that which has taken place in all the history of the Christian Church. The disciples had been used to seeing Jesus heal disease; but now they were outside of Judaism, and they were not able, in their narrow circumstances, to think that Jesus could possibly help this poor woman, His disciples came beseeching Him, and saying, " Send her away, for she crieth after us ".

How strange it was! As if Jesus was not in the world to be cried after! As if it was not the very thing the soul of Jesus desired—that men should cry after Him. How strange that those nearest Him and most full of His Spirit, who, in a few short years, were to be the commissioned representatives of their Master, should have thought it an enormity and not right that human souls, in their need, should cry after the Divine Redeemer.

My dear friends, if we have ever narrowed ourselves and been unwilling to allow any approach of the soul of man to the soul of God except according to the modes which we have laid down, has there not been simply repeated over again that which took place on the coasts of Tyre and Sidon when the disciples tried to drive the poor appealing woman away from her Lord? " Send her away, for she crieth after us!" So the Church has again and again said of some wild cry outside her borders. When the Church has tried to silence any unchurchly ways in which the human soul has appealed to God, it has been the disciples over again trying to send the woman away.

There is no tolerance of that with Jesus. He did not encourage what His disciples said. He condemns them by His silence, as afterwards He condemned them by His spoken word. Whatever the mission of the Church of Christ may be, however blessed her ordinances and her ministrations, she loses the value of her ordinances and her ministrations, or diminishes dreadfully the value of them all, if she remonstrates at any cry outside herself by which the soul of man is trying to come to God; though it be in any heathen religion, in any outreach of the soul from its darkness, any irrepressible cry of the human soul towards its Redeemer.

Then, what is the objection that Jesus made? I think it is interesting: " I am not sent but unto the lost sheep of the house of Israel ". He recognised the value of positive institutions and distinct arrangements. And it is good that they should be recognised. It is good that the soul of man should proceed under certain regulations; and this truth of which I have been speaking, that there is an immediate access of the soul to God, that does not remove the legitimate and healthy value that belongs to the Church's rites and ceremonies. Do you remember how Jesus used some special form or method in order that He might impress the great spiritual principle upon the mind of those who were speaking to Him? How He sent back the man who had been healed of the leprosy to the priest, in order that the cure might be legitimately registered? How He told the blind man to go and wash in the pool of Siloam? Methods were continually used by Jesus. He could not and would not make Himself the slave of His methods; but He would use them and recognise their worth. You or I may not say: "Because there is immediate access of the human soul to God; because, without baptism or confirmation or communion, I may come directly to my Heavenly Father, therefore these things are of no consequence, and I will not use them". That is not the spirit of Jesus. To keep them in their true use, recognise how, for substantiating the perpetual life of humanity, they are of use; for making vivid and distinct personal experience they are of use; but at the same time, let not ourselves, let not the Church, be made their slaves. That, it seems to me, is the lesson of the conversation of Jesus with the Canaanitish woman.

To keep the fundamental spiritual truth that man stands in immediate communion with his God, and at the same time keep the sense of the value of the means of grace and the methods of Christian ministrations, that would not seem to be so difficult as it has proved to be.

The world has had these two great classes which

have proved the difficulty—men seeking God, and finding God, but making their very hold on God less effective because they would have nothing to do with the organised Church; on the other hand, men so wrapped up with the organised Church that they have made what ought to be a help toward God into a cloud hovering between their soul and Him.

How the woman seems to have understood it all! She heard what Jesus said, and did not attempt to excuse herself or enlarge her claim. The beauty of this woman's character is the humanity in her love that pierced through every difficulty, even through the difficulty that came from the Lord Himself. She did not attempt to argue that she belonged to the children of Israel. She simply repeated her cry: " Lord, help me! "

O soul, for which there seems to be no place within the Christian churches, that has not been trained or inducted into the organisations of Christianity, if the Church seems dead to you, and her ceremonies do not seem to answer your needs, then cry, " Lord, help me! " Claim your help in the pity of the Father. Be the Canaanitish woman for the moment; be an outsider, if you will; but cry to God. You can come, you must come, directly to His soul, for you are His child. Do not go away uncomforted and unhealed because the churches seem to have no satisfaction or relief for you. God is yours, and you are

God's, whatever your sins and whatever your woes.

The psychology of the reluctance of Jesus to answer this woman's prayer sometimes suggests a great many thoughts, and sometimes leads us, it seems to me, somewhat astray. We have heard people say, again and again, that the reluctance in this case, the reason for its being manifested is that the faith of the person may be tested and increased. It always seems to me that there is something not thoroughly truthful in such a motive, something, therefore, which we cannot really associate with Jesus. No! There was a genuine reason. Jesus' work was proceeding in a certain method. He could depart from that method, but He must depart for a reason. When a departure was suggested, the first thing that came up to Him was the great law and purpose of His life. It was only when the reason became very strong that He was willing to depart. It would seem that there was a necessity for adhering to the ordinary course of His work, yet not an absolute but a relative necessity, which could be surpassed, but had first to be moved aside by reason.

God makes use of a great many regulations which He does not primarily establish. Take the most extreme of all. A man falls into sin and lives a wretched life. After years, he repents of that life and comes to Jesus, and enters with abject penitence into his Saviour's grace. We know well enough how often the grace seems to be rich in proportion to the sin the man has passed through. What shall we say? Did God assent to the sin in order that the forgiveness might have this supreme preciousness? Not so. The sin came by the perverseness of the man's own will, as sin can only come. It came against the remonstrance of God's Spirit. It was only that Christ used it afterward in order that He might make out of it a more complete redemption. When we are met with the difficulty which Paul encountered centuries ago, and of which he speaks in one of his epistles, "What shall we say then? Shall we continue in sin that grace may abound? God forbid!" we are to remember that it is a dreadful thing to go into wilful sin; yet we are to remember that there is a power that can make, even out of that very sin, a richer and a deeper holiness. That is the mystery of the grace of God. There comes the suggestion to a great many minds, "Why not sin, in order that redemption may be more glorious?" Paul has answered that, "God forbid!" The solution of the riddle is that the soul which really desires God and anticipates redeeming grace cannot enter into willing sin. There are no such bargains and compromises to be made in order to get to God, because the soul that really desires to get to God is incapable of any bargains and compromises.

Observe the wit and wisdom of the woman! "Yea, Lord; yet the dogs eat of the crumbs that fall from the children's table." There is absolute humility and complete innocence. She does not care to rival her claims against the claims of the chosen people. She does not care whether she is going to get more or less than others of the grace of Christ. She simply knows she wants this and she must have it. "Anything, anything for me, so long as it can heal my child!" We find men matching their privileges against one another, wondering whether the old Jews had more privileges than the modern Gentiles, the Roman Catholics than the Protestants, whether this man, because of his peculiar doctrines, has an advantage over other men. The Canaanitish woman does not care what the children of Israel have. She simply says, "There must be enough left for me".

Then the Lord gave way. "Be it unto thee even as thou wilt." There is no withheld mercy that the soul requires which is not waiting simply for the opportunity to abandon itself in the utter bestowal of its grace upon the needy soul. Persevere, even if you have pleaded for years and seemed to get no entrance into the ear of God. The man, wrestling with the burden of this life and finding it too heavy, who by-and-by kills himself because he thinks there is no salvation at the hands of God, how cowardly his conduct is, and how poor it is, beside the impetuous faith with which this poor woman wrestles with the stone athwart the torrent of the mercy of her God, until by-and-by it is turned away and the torrent pours itself into the help of her need!

You say: " Will it be to-night, to-morrow, next year?" I don't know. Who can know? Who wants to know? Who has a right to want to know anything except the infinite love and infinite power of Christ, the Son of God? When I know that, then I am content.

I will not say it makes no difference. Every one clamours that the burden of sin may be lifted or the weight of sorrow eliminated now. But we can wait. And if we wait, even until the river has been crossed, and we enter into the light where there can be no darkness and the joy where there can be no pain, what matters it? Time is short and eternity is long, and Christ is the Lord of both.

THE REWARDS OF VICTORY.

"He that overcometh shall inherit all things."—REV. xxi. 7.

I THINK it is always exceedingly interesting to remember that the Bible closes with a great outburst of hope and courage. From the time of its beginning with the Book of Genesis on through all the books in the ages that have come between, there have been a multitude of strains of great music in the Bible. Sometimes there are strains of earnest and serious rebuke, sometimes of earnest and faithful exhortation, sometimes a recital of duty in the calmest and simplest way. Sometimes there are verses, and chapters, and periods of history, which, if we take them by themselves, would seem almost to leave mankind to the most hopeless discouragement. There have been chapters on which the most pessimistic theories have been built. But it is certainly interesting to remember that when the Bible gathers itself up for its great close—for although the Book of Revelation was not the last of the books of the Bible which was written, it holds its true place at the close of the great Bible history—when we come to gather up the whole of God's message to the world in the Bible its strain is unbroken peace, comfort, and encouragement. It comes to man's soul with a great outbreak of hope and glory. It is almost as if there had been long consultation and communion between dear friends. During the years in which they have been in intercourse with one another, into how many different relationships they have entered, and how many words have passed between them! But there comes at last a moment when they are to separate for a time, when the special association and the constant communication are to be broken; and we all know how rich and precious are words spoken then, how significant they become of the whole relationship that exists between the two souls, and how we are continually looking back to those last words that have been spoken, not merely the words spoken again and again in the ordinary intercourse of life, but to words spoken then, when life has seemed to gather itself up in the fulness and richness of its meaning. So the Bible gathers itself together, and says these great rich words which are in the inspiring chapters of the Book of the Revelation of St. John. I ask you to take one of these verses this morning for a little while. It seems to me that there are no words that one who has but few chances of speaking to this company of his fellow-men can speak from more simply and earnestly than some of these words that have in them the whole spirit of our Christian faith, the whole spirit of the relationship between God and man.

The words I have quoted are words that correspond to many others which are to be found in the Book of Revelation—promises to him that overcometh. I ask at once what is meant by the overcoming that is spoken of again and again in the earlier chapters as well as in this later chapter of the great Book ? You remember how frequently the word occurs in the epistles to the different churches in the second and third chapters of the Revelation of St. John—" To him that overcometh ". Overcometh what? There is no special difficulty, there is no peculiar struggle of life spoken of. It takes life as a trial, and represents the great relationship which man is to hold to life. He that overcometh, not this or that special difficulty, nor this or that peculiar struggle in which he is engaged, but he that in his whole life comes forth as victor, not as vanquished, as one who has overcome, not who has been overcome—it is to him that the great promises are given in the earlier and later chapters of the Book of Revelation. And we recognise at once, and think something which occurs to us in all our observation of the world, in all the experience of our life—the way in which man is either overcome by this world or overcomes this world. Either it becomes his master, or it becomes his slave ; he gets it under his feet, or is trampled under its feet. It is so in reference to every special experience of life, and in reference to all life as a whole. Take a man in his business: by-and-by, as the years go on, he becomes either the servant of his business, or the master of his business; either it makes him its slave, bringing him down to its level, or he makes it his slave, compelling it to render force to his character, and make him even a better and a stronger man. Take a man in his profession: no matter how liberal his idea of his profession, he is capable of becoming its slave, of being brought down to its meanest drudgeries and most mercenary motives, or he is capable of making his occupation, his profession, his servant, compelling it to render strength to his character, and to give power to him by which he may serve his fellow-men. Take every experience of life, take every joy of life: a man either becomes the slave of joy and prosperity, being made self-conceited by it, or he becomes the master of his prosperity and joy, compelling it to render richness to his character, to mellow his whole life into a fuller and deeper relationship to God. And even more with regard to sorrow than with regard to joy. I see my fellow-man who comes into suffering and distress; my anxiety for him is to know whether he is going, by-and-by, to have his sorrow under his feet, or, rather, to have it at his side as his servant, to help him in every way to be a richer, a greater, a more godly man, or whether he is, by-and-by, to become brutal, and sour, and cynical, and complaining because of the suffering that God has sent him, making it his devil instead of his angel, drawing forth from it poison instead of real, helpful food. So with regard to every experience of life ; and is it not so with regard to life as a whole ? I see two of my fellow-men, I see their bodies laid in the grave at last after the work of life is over, after their experience is past. I stand by as the dust of these worn out bodies is laid in the ground ; the struggle of this life is over, their souls have passed forward into the mysterious experiences that lie where a man's eye cannot see. How different is my feeling with regard to the two men. One I call a failure, but as to the other, it seems to me almost as if the funeral chants were an outburst of triumphant joy, as if, when we followed in the procession to the grave, we were following the victor up to the capitol, and rejoicing that he was allowed to conquer in the struggle of life. We do not know what may be beyond, what new experiences, what other trials, what other chances and new opportunities may be offered to the soul that has failed in this world, but we do know that there are failures in this world and we do know that there are successes. You know I am not talking about the man who makes money or who fails to make money, about the man who attracts or fails to attract the observation of his fellow-man, but about the man who has become the master or has become the slave of this world, which may either be master or slave to him who rules it or is ruled by it. He that overcometh and he that has been overcome, how well we know them both, how people sometimes seem to be the overcomers by the side of one that has been overcome, and how clear the mark of the overcomer is, how immediately we recognise who has conquered the world, and who has been conquered by it, and how, more than that, we feel that even, although the men that are overcome are counted by millions, and the men who overcome the world and make it their slave, seem to be few among their fellows, yet these are the true lives, and the only true lives! And every man has it in his power to conquer the world, for man is stronger than circumstance, because man is the child of God, and circumstance is only the arrangement of God for the service, the development, and education of His children.

I said that these words, "he that overcometh," and the promises made to him that overcometh, occur again and again in the Book of Revelation, and I think it will be interesting just to observe several of the passages in which the word occur, and see what some of these prerogatives are that are given to the man who overcomes the world. What I want you especially to notice is the essentialness of these promises, that they are not simply promises made of special gifts that God has arbitrarily attached to the overcoming of the world, to the living a noble, a manly, and a masterful life, but they are essentially united to such a life. A man could not live such a life without those promises coming and being fulfilled to him. Do you remember that in the second chapter of the Book of Revelation, the promise is made to the church of Ephesus, " To him that overcometh will I give to eat of the tree of life"? See what the promise is. Man's life seems to die out in death; to him that overcometh the world there shall be given a vitality that goes beyond this world. It is in virtue of man's power to overcome this world that he lays hold upon immortality. The reason why man, in spite of every discouragement, in spite of disease, and death, and the grave, has so inextinguishable a belief in the immortality of life, is the mastery which he has had over this life. If all men had been slaves of circumstances, mankind never could have believed in immortality. It is because man has proved his power to conquer circumstances that he has believed ultimately in his power to conquer that last great circumstance, and believed that death was nothing but an event, an experience in life. To him that overcometh it is given to eat of the tree of life, and to know himself immortal.

And there is another promise made to the same church at Ephesus in the same chapter, where it is said " he that overcometh shall not be hurt of the second death ". There is the same promise made negatively that was made positively in the earlier part of the epistle to the church at Ephesus —" Shall not be hurt of the second death ". Man looks beyond death, and he knows that that is not the end; there is something, he cannot tell what, which is beyond. The future world is peopled not simply with hopes, but with fears also. Things that will hurt souls as well as things that will delight and enrich souls are to come with that great mysterious world that lies beyond the grave. What is the promise made to him who has conquered this world by the strength of God, who has lived a masterful, manly life? It is not that the curtain is drawn back and everything is shown to him in the everlasting world, and how he is going to be able to conquer everything; but it is all grouped into one great danger, and it is said that he who in this world has lived strong in the strength of God shall be equal to it all; he shall not be hurt by anything that is there. And so the man who has trusted and assimilated the strength of God in this world lies down to die, and his friends say to him: " Are you afraid of what will come to you upon the other side?" And he says: " No; I have so trusted and appropriated the strength of God here that I feel in all my nature that this strength is enough for everything that shall come beyond. I cannot be hurt by it. I do not know what it is. Nothing can hurt the child of God to whom the Father has proved Himself so near." That is the first promise, then, in these two passages—the promise of inextinguishable vitality and security.

Then see the rich promise made in this same chapter of the Book of Revelation, in the epistle to the Church at Pergamos, one of the richest epistles in all these earliest chapters. "To him that overcometh will I give to eat of the hidden manna, and will give him a white stone, and in the stone a new name written, which no man knoweth saving he that receiveth it." Think of the mystic beauty of that promise. There shall be given to each soul a token of secret relationship between it and God, giving to every nature something that is so peculiarly its own that it shall be like the hidden manna coming direct out of the hand of God into the heart that receives it. There shall be given the white stone with a new name that no one can read save the soul and God who gives the stone. It is not merely the vast general relationship which mankind hold to their Father—that is not enough for the soul of man; but as man overcomes the world, as he grows into a deeper and deeper sense of God's power appropriated and made his, there comes a sweet, a deep, an awful, a mystic sense of how God belongs to him and he belongs to God. The two are not simply united together by the great chains that bind the Creator to His creation, the father to the family, but every soul has its own personal knowledge of God as its God, and knows that in the heart of God there is a chamber where its name is written and where its throne is set. Poor, very poor, is the Christian life that knows nothing of that experience. Very weak and meagre is that resting upon God, which merely knows Him as the great Providential Ruler of the world, and has never, in any rich, exalted moment, appropriated the certain sense that there is in God a love that is entirely its own, a manna upon which no other soul can feed, a stone with its name written upon it which no other eyes can understand. My friends, do you know anything of that experience? If not, there is the richest chamber of all the Christian life before you yet. Press forward and occupy it.

Then remember another promise made in the other chapter of the Book of Revelation, in the epistle to the church at Sardis: " He that overcometh, the same shall be clothed in white raiment ". All the other promises seem to be something given to the soul. Here is something that is so absolutely a part of the soul that it is spoken of as the very clothing of the soul—innocency. After all there is no gift that can be given to a man that is satisfactory or sufficient until we come to character. There is nothing that God can endow a nature with, that can be the fullest satisfaction of His nature, until God puts His own innocency, His own incapacity of sin, into a human heart, and makes it pure with His purity, white with His whiteness, and so even richer than the promise of intimate mystic communion with God. There is the promise of the very transference of the life of God into our life, so that we shall become incapable of sin, as He is incapable of sin, and walk with Him in a whiteness that shall be like His own. These are the great promises of character.

And then you remember another promise to the church of Philadelphia, also in the third chapter of the Book of Revelation, where it is said : " Him that overcometh will I make a pillar in the temple of My God "—the temple of God which is the rich structure of God's eternal purpose. When everything alters, that stands firm ; whatever changes come, there is no change there. Now, to know that your life or my life may be put as an element into that eternity—that because we are true, and faithful, and upright, and strong by God's strength, the world may be made more substantial, and God's promise more eternal because we have lived—to feel that the integrity of our life may be contributed as a portion of the great integrity and perpetuity of the universe—is there any promise that can be greater than that ?

Other promises might seem to have something of the selfish about them—vitality, communion, a full character, and innocency : all this belongs to the soul ; but the soul that is faithful to God, and rejoices in His strength, and overcomes by Him, makes the universe stronger. Poor is the man that cannot take that promise to His soul and feel how rich it is!

Then just one more. In the same third chapter of the Book of Revelation there is a promise made to the church at Laodicea: "To him that overcometh will I grant to sit with Me in My throne, even as I also overcame, and am set down with My Father in His throne". To sit upon the throne of Jesus, to be like Jesus, the Judge of the World, to help to establish those standards by which other people shall shape their lives, to help to make the faith of other people, who shall live in years after we are dead and forgotten, stronger, more capable of knowing the truth, more capable of doing right because we have lived—that is to sit with Jesus upon His throne and to judge the world. Do you not know men in your own circles who judge the world in which they live, who establish standards to which other people turn to know whether their acts and thoughts are wrong or right? Is it not a great thing to know that we, overcoming by the strength of God, may do something of that kind for all the world that is to come after us,' and that hence men may know what is right, and be able to do what is right, more truly because of our forgotten lives? Lost we shall be in the great multitude, but the standards of mankind will be higher because of our faithful lives.

Group, then, these promises in your imagination, think of them as they heap themselves one upon another, as they come in glorious procession —the promise of vitality, the promise of personal communion with the infinite, eternal, living God, the promise of a great share of His character, of a growing purity and whiteness, the promise of a part in the stability of the universe, the promise of a share in the judgment of the world and the shaping of its standards. All these, as I have said, are promises essentially; they are not something taken out of a treasury from which God might have taken something else to give to the soul, but they are promises essentially, they are the inevitable consequences of that struggle to overcome the world which is simply the recognition by man that God has made him, as it were, the master, and not the slave, of the things with which he has to deal. And so it belongs to all alike; it belongs to every life, to every struggle. He who comes out of any temptation victor brings all these things with him. He who fights in any special skirmish in the great long campaign, and comes forth master and not conquered, begins to have something of the fulfilment of this promise already. No man ever fought with any special sin and overcame it, no man ever set himself against any temptation to do wrong and did right in spite of the temptation, that it did not give to him a larger vitality, an increased intercourse and communion with God, a richer power of character in his own life, that he did not add something to the stability of the universe, that he did not help to judge the world and lift its standards.

I see the same power still given out after years and years in the chamber of sickness and suffering: the wrestling hands that have been there in silence; the hours of darkness in which the soul has struggled to take hold of God, and not abjure and desert its faith. Oh, the times when the soul has been tempted to curse God and die, and has refused, and blessed God and lived! And at the last, when the sickness is over and the soul comes out, it matters not whether into renewed communication with men here in this world, or into the painless glory of the world that is to come, must it not carry with it these great things—a great vitality, a true communion with the infinite God, a real character in its own life, an additional force that has added to the universe's stability, a higher standard given to the actions of mankind?

There are, too, active as well as passive trials. So with the temptation of the young man who fights with his lusts, his temptations to intemperance, his temptations to a low, degraded, and mercenary life, and he comes out determined that whatever happens to him in the world he will be pure and will be useful. Let the determination be absolutely made, let the victory over his temptation be won, and these things are in his soul; he has overcome, and there has been given to him to eat of the tree of life, and he is not afraid that anything can hurt him in this world or in the world to come; and he has the hidden manna and the precious stone, and is walking perpetually in white with God ; he is a pillar in the temple of God, and he sits on the throne of Jesus Christ. They are not too great words, my friends ; they are not too great words, young man, for you to take as the promises of your life. Believe that they shall be given to you if, by the strength of God, you overcome.

Look at the life of Him, the young Man, who with His Divine humanity, stands perpetually, not merely as a hopeless standard which we never shall attain, but as the proper pattern and prospect of our lives—look at the life of Jesus Christ, a life of overcoming, a life of struggle, a life of victory, a life of everyday claims and promises, a life which, at the last, will reach out its hands and take those promises in their fulness to His heart. Every one of the promises that I have told you of, every one of these inevitable consequences which pursue the man who really overcomes by God's strength, came to Jesus Christ. Did not He eat of the fruit of the tree of life? Can He possibly be thought of as being hurt by the second death ? Had He not the hidden manna and the precious stone always? Was He not always walking in white with God ? Was He not a very pillar—nay, the central pillar —that held the roof of this earthly temple of God ?

And did not He sit upon the throne, and does He not sit upon the throne for ever, establishing the standards and judging the lives of men? He is perfectly that which we approach little by little, for He has graciously set His life, not merely as the Saviour-life, by which, as from above, we are lifted up to unapproachable heights, but He has set His life also as a brother-life, taking the hand of which we may go forward from strength to strength, until within that range which belongs to His life and to our life we may come to be entirely like Him.

Remember that in all I have been saying to you this morning there is no question about great and little lives. It seems to me, when I think about the lives of people that live in this world, that in one sense they are so little, and in another sense they are so great, that all distinctions of littleness and greatness really pass away. These questions of the motives of the lives that shall be lived are not questions of the quantity of life, but of the quality of life. The meanest, the littlest life must live by the same high motives as the greatest and most splendid life. And so to every one, however small may seem his task, however full of drudgery may seem his duties, however circumscribed his lot, it is possible either to overcome or to be overcome; and if he overcomes, all these great promises shall come to the humblest and to the most limited of us all as truly as to the greatest and most enlarged.

What is it to overcome? I began by telling you and I close by telling you; it is to know that the one great power that is in this universe is our power. We talk about power, and men may grow conceited as they lift themselves up and say: "I will be strong and conquer the world". Ah! it is not to be done so. There is one real and true strength in this universe, and that is God's strength, and no man ever did any strong thing yet that God did not do that strong thing in him. A man makes himself full of strength only as the trumpet makes itself full, by letting it be held at the lips of the trumpeter: so only man lets himself be made strong as he lets himself be held in the hand of God. As the chisel is powerless—if it tries to carve a statue by itself it goes tumbling and stumbling over the precious surface of the stone—as the chisel becomes itself filled and inspired with genius when it is put into the hand of the artist, so man, putting himself into the hand of God, loses his awkwardness as well as his feebleness, and becomes full of the graciousness and the strength of the perfect nature. And to put myself into the hands of God, what does that mean? To know that God is my Father, to know that my life is a true issuing in this world of His life, to know that I become myself only as I know myself His child. So the soul puts itself into the soul of God, and lets God do its work, through Him, so that that great mysterious consciousness enters into the life which was in Paul's life. Do you remember, " I live, yet not I, but Christ liveth in me"? So the soul which has given itself to God in filial consecration, says : " I live, yet not I, but God liveth in me". As the child in the household does not know whether the things that he does from hour to hour are his things or his father's things, so does his father's will and law fill the whole household with its inspiration. Know God your Father ; recognise what your baptism means, that it was the claiming of your soul for the Father-soul of God ; give yourself to Him in absolute, loving obedience. Do not think about it as an unnatural thing, as a strange thing for a man to do, to give himself to God. The strange thing is that any man or woman should be living in the world without being given to, or filled with God. Give yourself to Him, as the child gives himself to the father, as the most natural and true thing in all your life ; and then, His power glowing through your power, the world shall become yours as it is His, and in overcoming you shall inherit all things—inherit, because they are your Father's, so they shall become yours. The little miserable relations in which we live, the way in which we determine to be strong here and strong there, when the real secret of life is to put ourselves into the power of the Eternal Strength, to know God our Father—nay, in the strong words of Scripture, to *make* God our Father, by knowing that He is our Father, and then through Him to overcome. May God grant it for us all!—in different ways, of course. One man's fight and another man's fight may be entirely different, and yet there is the same great fight in life for all of us. May God grant us all to overcome, and so to receive these certain promises!

ST. PAUL AT PHILIPPI.

"Therefore, my brethren dearly beloved and longed for, my joy and crown, so stand fast in the Lord, my dearly beloved."—PHILIPPIANS iv. 1.

It is good for us to bring together the story of Paul's life found in the Acts and compare it with the Epistles. The history throws light on the correspondence. We see how he came to feel as he did towards the Philippians. But even if we had no record in the Acts of the visit to Philippi, it would not be difficult to characterise this Epistle. It seems to have, above all the other Epistles, its own peculiar character.

It is not, indeed, marked by theological roots, like the Epistle to the Romans. It has not the intense religious life of the Epistle to the Colossians. It has not the fire and zeal of the Epistle to the Galatians. It does not enter into the examination of special circumstances, like the Epistle to the Corinthians. But it contains a revelation of the richness and completeness of St. Paul's own life as it is revealed in no other. If we were to examine the correspondence which any man had with his fellow-men, each letter might be likened to a window of coloured glass, each window with glass of a different colour from the rest. Every letter would allow us to see, through its own peculiar medium, some character or mood or condition of the writer. And thus we might come to one letter which would be like a window of pure white glass, letting in the light as if there were no glass there, or only with such added brilliancy as the glass might give to it. So, in the Epistle to the Philippians, we see St. Paul, not under particular circumstances of excitement or provocation, but simply as he was, as his friends knew him, as he was simply at his best. It was the first of the Epistles which he wrote after his captivity at Rome. It was written under circumstances which recalled his first visit to Philippi, and the dear friends and dear friendships he made there.

There must always have remained in his mind a wonderful interest in the incidents of that journey, when he crossed the water and passed from Asia into Europe, and saw, for the first time, that great Continent, in which the religion of Christ has since spread so widely and so deeply, and in such majestic forms.

At Philippi he found a little company of people willing to listen to him. Especially there was one, a woman, who was impressed by his teaching, and became a convert to the truth, and asked him to make her house his home. Then came the tumult in the streets, and, by-and-by, the imprisonment, and the conversion of the gaoler. The gaoler had asked that great question which St. Paul was so glad to have the world ask, which it seemed to him the world must ask. It is the one typical instance in Scripture. The question was asked out of an anxious heart. It came from a voice all intent with anxiety to one who was able to answer it. And the answer was returned to a soul that was able to understand it just because the soul was so anxious. St. Paul had united himself with the Philippians because he found them so very teachable. He passed from Philippi to Athens and to Corinth. But nowhere else had he found souls so apt to be taught, and to whom he fastened himself with such sincere and personal affection.

Epaphroditus had been sent by the Church at Philippi with supplies for St. Paul's necessities, and had fallen sick. He had been restored in answer to the Apostle's prayers. Then he had been employed by St. Paul to do missionary work, which it was impossible for St. Paul himself to do in his imprisonment. And now Epaphroditus was about to return to Philippi. By him was sent this letter, in which St. Paul pours out his heart to the church which had so remembered him in his captivity.

In these facts you get the keynote of the epistle. It is simply running over with light and joyousness. If there be one word which can describe it in distinction from all the rest of the epistles, that one word is "*joy*". "*Rejoice in the Lord always. And again I say, rejoice.*" "*But I rejoiced in the Lord greatly.*" "*Finally, my brethren, rejoice in the Lord.*" Such is the note of the Epistle to the Philippians.

He has not, as in other epistles, to rebuke those whom he addresses for shortcomings and backslidings. He has simply to rejoice with them in the persistency of their faith, and to bid them go on in the way in which they are going.

The way in which he was able, in the midst of discouragements and fears, to give himself up to his joy is a most characteristic thing. There is no shadow in any part of this epistle.

It is a great thing for a man to be joyous who really understands this world. The joyousness of a little child who merely grasps the sunlight, oblivious of the darkness which has been and must be again, means little. It is a spontaneous and beautiful thing, but it signifies little as to the real character of human life. But when a man goes through what St. Paul did, he understands better than any other man what this world is. It is not a sign of greatness for a man to be despondent. It is a sign of sensitiveness, but not of the deepest sensitiveness. The deepest sensitiveness sees behind all the wickedness of men the unchangeable riches of the grace of God, and so is happy among things which, seen by themselves, are full of sadness.

Many of the noblest men of our time are silent, because they know no good word to say about the century in which they live. They are ready to confess the marvellous progress that has been made along the lines of human knowledge, and power, and greatness. And yet there loom up great fears, such as have not been in the hearts of men before. No man can be in sympathy with this nineteenth century, and not be in sympathy with the deep sadness that ever lies, with pressing burden, upon many of its best and truest hearts. It is good to take a wide view of the world, and to be in sympathy with all the great movements that are going on in the world, and which makes this age in advance of all the ages that have been before. But there is to come a great century, by the power of God, filled with His Spirit, recognising just as deeply as ours the interests of humanity, but which still shall be filled with a joyousness like that of St. Paul. Take the man who understands best the wants of humanity to-day, and St. Paul shall stand beside him and shall show that he understands them vastly more deeply. It is wonderful for any human soul to live in this century and breathe the atmosphere by which he is surrounded. St. Paul knew all that as well as any poet or prophet of our time.

One cause of his joyousness is his unselfishness. He knew that any day, after a hasty trial, he might be led forth from prison to death. But he had no fear of that. He lost himself and looked abroad, thankful for the little company of disciples at Philippi. And yet there is no Epistle so absolutely full of the circumstances of St. Paul himself. Every verse opens the door of the gaol and lets us see the poor prisoner. We can feel it written by a hand that has a fetter on it.

There is something very fine about the way in which he is able to pour himself into the Epistle and all the while be unselfish. There is a certain sort of unselfishness which tries to be self-effacing. A man says, " Let me forget myself, let me cease to remember the burdens lying upon me, let me identify myself with those to whom I am speaking as if I were living their lot ". It is a good effort, but there is something better. St. Paul has an exquisite way of remembering his circumstances, and, from the standpoint of his circumstances, helping his brothers with his sympathy. To be ourselves, and to speak of ourselves, not in self-congratulation or in appeal for sympathy, but, whether prosperous or miserable, to rejoice because from that condition we can bring help to others—that is the highest unselfishness.

Are you learned or are you ignorant ? It matters not. The way to use either of the two conditions is not to pretend it does not exist, but to see that it is the starting-point of your life, and, with the distinct kind of power which it contributes to your vitality, give yourselves to the lives of other men and make them strong. Whatever kind of power we have, whether artistic or intellectual or practical, let us recognise ourselves, and not efface ourselves, recognising ourselves for the benefit of others and the glory of God.

There is a constant tendency among men, when they desire to reach others, to endeavour to efface themselves. The rich man thinks he must cast his riches into the sea before he can be in full sympathy with the poor man. The poor man thinks he must leave his poverty behind him and become somewhat artificially rich. The learned man thinks he must consider himself ignorant; and the ignorant man thinks he must conceal his ignorance. But true unselfishness starts distinctly from, and never forgets, itself. It is full of self-consciousness. Something keeps it from being a stagnant pool, and turns it into a strong and vehement river, running on toward its purpose and carrying its own distinct contribution to that purpose. St. Paul never ceases to feel the presence of the gaoler by his side, but always he was conscious of that which God had given him through his imprisonment.

There is something wonderfully pure about the joy of St. Paul, and the purity lies in the constant consciousness of two things; first, *God above him*; second, *his brethren around him*. The way to purify every joy is to lift it up; not simply to be happy because our circumstances are happy, but to rejoice that by our circumstances we are glorifying God and may help our brethren. A man to-day becomes a wonderfully happy man when his happiness comes pouring from the skies like a great shower, and rising from the ground like a great fountain. When a man stands in the simple consciousness of happiness and says, "How happy I am!" then his happiness is in danger of corruption. If it remains simply conscious happiness it turns to corruption. But if he immediately says, "Here is God glorifying Himself in the world by another happy life, and my happiness may fall upon my brethren with some mitigation of their lives," then his happiness is kept pure.

Oh, my dear friends! It may well be some of you here to-night, young or old, have to-day realised some happiness. Let it summon you to think of the hand from which it comes, as the flower might be supposed to drink in the sunshine and think more of the glory of the sun than of the beauty and brightness itself has received.

There is in this Epistle one strain of anxiety, which shows how anxiety may exist in the happiest lot. In the beginning of the second chapter he writes: "*If, therefore, there be any consolation in Christ, if any comfort of love, if any fellowship of the Spirit, if any bowels and mercies, fulfil ye my joy, that ye be like minded, having the same love, being of one accord, of one mind. Let nothing be done through strife or vainglory, but in lowliness of mind let each esteem the other better than themselves."* He feared some sort of dissension and difficulty. The church was full of vitality—the best condition a church could have. But he feared their very richness of spiritual life might bring them to criticisms of one another, and narrowness, in which some individual should think his type of piety ought to be the type of all. How natural it is! We picture to ourselves a church overrunning with life, full of zeal and work, and looking forward to richer enjoyments of the Master's love. Just in proportion to zeal is likely to come division and narrowness. Every soul in such a church is likely to consider its way the better way, if not the only way. Such a spirit is likely to grow in a live church, and less likely to grow in a partly dead church. Many of the largest spiritual conditions of the Church have had seeds and roots of bitterness and sectarianism and dictation, by which they have lost that great peculiar richness of the Christian Church by which every soul develops in a different way. It was a deep, a sad, and a natural anxiety of St. Paul's.

Be sure to live so deeply in such consciousness of the spring and source of all spiritual life that no difference in the development of the life shall keep you from recognising it in another. And this can only be done by feeling the roots of the diversified life of the Church to be in Him who is the Head of the Church.

In the first chapter is another characteristic

passage. He is speaking of the way in which every one of them is to be humble in criticism of his brethren. "*Let this mind be in you which was also in Christ Jesus, Who, being in the form of God, thought it not robbery to be equal with God.*" The new version more correctly translates, "*Being in the essential nature of God, thought it not a thing to be aspired after to be equal with God*". In His incarnation He abandoned equality with God. He did not go up and sit by the side of God. He took upon himself the nature and reputation and came in the likeness of man. He humbled Himself and became obedient unto death.

The point is this : The way in which St. Paul, when he is teaching the Philippians—who were, after all, commonplace people, such as he might have found anywhere in Macedonia, or in any village in the world—the duties and simple details of daily life, sets before them the highest of all patterns. He does not say, " This man, or that man, is to be your example ". He wants a star to set before them, by whose shining they are to guide their lives, towards whose shining they are to direct their steps. He does not lift up a light for them, he brings down the light for them out of the very skies. There is nothing in the heavens, or in Deity itself, too good to become the pattern of the humblest soul in Philippi taught by St. Paul.

In these verses we have one of the most remarkable and beautiful descriptions of the Incarnation.

It is rich in theology. It is rich because it is not a great, formal statement, as if he took his seat in a lecture-room and there expounded the doctrine —where he would be sure to get it wrong. It is the richest and deepest description of the nature of Jesus Christ which we have, to which the well-instructed student of the New Testament would turn first of all, in which the mystery of the Incarnation is most unfolded, as if to set before the eyes and hearts of simple men and women the nature of Christ, that He might be the pattern of their lives.

In St. Paul, the theologian is never separate and distinct. He is never the didactic, autocratic teacher. He is always the sympathising brother.

THE EPISTLE TO THE COLOSSIANS.

" Paul, an apostle of Jesus Christ by the will of God, and Timotheus our brother, to the saints and faithful brethren in Christ which are at Colosse.—COL. i. 1, 2.

THE Epistle to the Colossians differs strikingly from that to the Philippians. Much of the interest of the Epistle to the Philippians depends on the Apostle's relations to that Church, which he loved with especial fondness. But St. Paul never visited Colosse, and never saw the faces of the Christians there. Hence these two Epistles show us the difference between what one writes to dear and trusted friends, and what the same man writes to people whom he has never seen, though he has certain interests in common with them. The Colossians could remember no days in which they sat under St. Paul's instructions. The tie between the writer and the readers of this Epistle was simply that the great principles of the Gospel which the Apostle was preaching had taken root in Colosse.

During St. Paul's imprisonment at Rome there had come to him one who had visited Colosse, and who brought an account of special corruptions that had crept into the Christianity of the Colossian believers. And this letter was written as a remonstrance against these corrupt teachings. It stands as a perpetual remonstrance against the same corruptions wherever they attempt to enter into the Christian Church.

How nobly the writer deals with the conditions he feels called upon to rebuke and to confute and to condemn! He goes out of his way to find everything he can possibly say with truthfulness of the excellency of the Colossian Christians' lives, and heaps all this together in the opening salutation. It is a noble specimen of controversial writing. When we feel called upon to blame people, we are so apt to fasten instantly and exclusively upon what we have to blame, and to forget how much good there is in them! We often seem to feel that those who differ from us within the Christian fold are further from us than if they were outside altogether. We may recognise something of this spirit in our own lives all the while. Those who have any great principles of agreement with us, but differ from us in certain respects, seem more worthy of denunciation than do those who are totally opposed to us. We ought to read such an epistle as this to the Colossians to learn how to deal generously with such people. St. Paul goes on to speak more unsparingly, but in a tone which must have awakened deep self-examination and regret for their errors, without provoking anger.

Colosse was one of a little group of great cities in Asia Minor. Laodicea, whose church was rebuked in Revelations, lay not far from Colosse. There is something of special interest in a church which seems to have grown up from wafted seeds blown abroad from one of the gardens of the Lord, which one of His gardeners had planted. In those days every disciple who had the Spirit of God in his heart, and believed in God with all his soul, sent from his own life influences which went out to the establishment of churches and the doing of untold good to the souls of men.

It was to the church at Colosse that St. Paul sent back Onesimus, the slave.

Let us try to see the condition of things in the church at the time when this epistle was written. Certain errors of doctrine had grown up out of the wilfulness of the teachers there. It is not easy for us to understand what the errors were, they belong so absolutely to the Eastern mind, and have such a different aspect and character for those who live in the West. By comparing this Epistle with that to the Romans, we shall see how different is the writing intended for the Eastern mind from the writing intended for the Western mind.

And yet, though we separate the world into East and West, it is one great world still. East and West belong to human nature. Questions arise both in the East and in the West which are stirring everywhere in human hearts. So the questions in the Church in Colosse belong to all time, belong right here in this distant place and these modern days.

One of the most interesting things in regard to the Christian religion is the way in which, as soon as it had outgrown Judaism, it came under the influence of the philosophic systems of the East. Those systems lacked the positive convictions which belonged to Western thought. But they carried their speculations up into the midst of supernal things.

There were *four ways* in which this influence manifested itself:—

1. *The Eastern mind continually tended to deal with supernal things not as related to the earth in which men were living, but as they exist absolutely, in themselves.* Not satisfied with feeling how the celestial arch of God's great nature bends over and involves all human life, they busied themselves with the region lying between human intelligence and the Deity. We can hardly conceive of the fascination such themes had for the early Christians and the distance such speculations seemed to put between man and God. People in their imagination thought that multitudes of beings and orders of beings, arranged in ranks until they reached God Himself, that hierarchies and principalities and powers filled all space. It is interesting to see how actively, carefully, systematically these ideas were set forth in their philosophy.

Where was Christ in all this multitude of being —He who had come to put into man's life the direct being of God? Lost in the midst of the myriads of existences, the body of emanations for ever coming off from the divine nature, Christ became so dim and impalpable, so etherealised, that it was impossible to behold Him. The air was so full of angelic ministries that He who was the great minister was lost in the multitude who shared the same nature as Himself.

2. *Asceticism.* The aim of asceticism is to mortify the body, to satisfy just as few as possible of its impulses and desires, to give it as little as possible to eat and drink, to make it sleep on as hard beds and walk on as hard roads as possible. Asceticism was running riot in the Colossian church. Everything belonging to this earth became debased and degraded; and especially the human body was regarded as the most miserable and contemptible of all things. It was taught that no man could be good in this bodily life. In reasoning of the life of Jesus on earth, they said that His body was not a real body, but only apparent; that what was crucified was not the real body of Christ. They reasoned in this way in order to still keep the notion that the body of man is a base and necessarily a degraded thing. Because the people could not help living upon the earth, they determined to live as meagre a life as possible.

3. *Formalism.* Asceticism is always closely connected with formalism. Where there is an attempt at separation from the body, as a despised and contemptible thing, there is a consequent limitation of the natural outflow of the religious spirit, and formalism, ritualism, ceremonialism, come as an artificial system to supply the place of the natural. This idea of the great richness of the spiritual life was not held broadly and generally, as it is good that men should hold it, but it was classified and specialised until they assumed to know everything about it.

4. In the fourth place, there was that which called for the warning against letting any man beguile them; "*intruding into those things which he hath not seen, vainly puffed up by his fleshly mind*". St. Paul, with profound philosophy, told them that this pseudo-spiritualism was not really spiritual at all, but came from their fleshly imagination. It was a morbid religion, unhealthy instead of healthy, formal and artificial instead of natural.

Religion, the power of salvation to the world, is the most natural thing that exists upon the earth. More than our political life, more than our social life filled with artificial conventionalities and hampering restrictions, the religious life is a natural thing—it is natural that man should be filled with God. Wherever any man has gone to Christ, as to a vague, mystic Being, instead of thinking of One Who, in our life, wrought out redemption, and showed that man might nobly live in a human body, by living in a human body Himself; wherever any man has tried to worship God by slavery to form, instead of making forms only the utterances of his own spiritual life—there has been a repetition of the corrupt Christianity in Colosse, fantastic and unhealthy.

There is a constant tendency to depart from the truth of the Gospel *on two sides.* On one side men say *that religion is too spiritual;* that there is not enough for our hands to do, not enough practical duties. These objectors would reduce Christianity down to a scheme of duties which might be written on tables and hung up on a wall. On the other side men say *that religion is not spiritual enough.* They ask us to see how it busies itself with things of this world, and ties itself to bodily conditions. We are bidden to look above the world, to leave our bodies behind, to mortify them until they have no power to hinder us from going to the heavens and dwelling with the angels. Far and wide on both sides of the great religion these departures extend. Some men would have all that is supernatural to be rejected. Others, like the Docetæ, would have us all the time revelling in thought among the things that belong to the skies.

What St. Paul brought to meet the corruptions of the Church in Colosse must be brought wherever formalism, asceticism, and contempt for the body creep into a church; wherever men dare to think that Christianity despises instead of honouring and exalting the body and all that belongs to it. It was perfectly clear that there was one great power which, if it could be brought to bear, would turn this fantastic religion out of doors and bring a natural religion into the Colossian Church. And that was the truth that Christ is the fulness of God; that the spiritual world is not peopled with multitudes of beings with whom we have to do; that we have not to go roaming about, asking after angels whose very existence is in our imagination —for Christ is "*the fulness of the Godhead bodily*". Whatever utterances are waiting, possibly, to be heard some time, the one great sufficient utterance is Jesus Christ, who came into the very centre of this life, and who not merely did not despise, but took possession of the human body, not merely in its best condition, but went with it to the Cross. Christ, the clear, palpable, distinct Christ, the child of Bethlehem and the man of Galilee—Christ crucified on Calvary, He is the redemption from all this mysticism and vagueness. Christ wrought in the midst of a human body, sanctified it by occupying it, and so treated it that, by-and-by, the Apostle could say, "*Know ye not that your bodies are the temples of the Holy Ghost?*" He sanctified everything that belongs to the body, breaking the bread which men love to eat, drinking the wine which men love to drink, weeping by the tomb where a body was buried, blessing the marriage where the children of men united themselves in the family life, declaring the thing to be done in this world was the redemption, and not the destruction, of this dear, familiar, human body.

There is a lesson in this for our own time. Jesus brought God down here, instead of flinging us into universal being to find God. Men are not to cast aside humanity and become misty angels. God calls on men and women to be men and women still, and to open their lives that they may be filled with the Deity. There are two great principles in the Gospel—*liberty* and *light*. " Live in *liberty* and *light*, not in slavery and darkness," is the perpetual exhortation of the Epistle to the Colossians. Live in liberty, using forms always as means, and not ends. Be ready to cast away forms as soon as they cease to secure the ends for which they were ordained. Look always behind the prohibition or injunction to that which the prohibition or injunction was intended to produce.

One striking instance, where the Apostle is made to teach a thing he intended to disown, is brought to our notice in the second chapter : " *Wherefore if ye be dead with Christ from the rudiments of the world, why, as though living in the world, are ye subject to ordinances (touch not : taste not : handle not : which all are to perish with the using), after the commandments and doctrines of men ?* " How many times do we hear this repeated, as if it were an injunction of the Bible, given somewhere—very few, I suppose, know that it comes from Colossians—whereas it is this very injunction which St. Paul is disowning. He is calling the people away from distinct, positive injunctions, such as this. He is urging them to live in freedom, by their own free will, since the world is not under law, but under grace. "*Touch not, taste not, handle not,*" St. Paul would have them understand, are injunctions from which, as injunctions, as commands laid upon them from outside, as mere rules of life, the Christian soul is free. Christianity replaces restraints like those by a nobler law. The soul which does not hear, ringing down from heaven, restraints against indulgences, by-and-by finds itself putting its own hand against the indulgence, by its own free will, and saying, "I will not touch, will not drink, will not handle". Here is liberty, here is true spiritual abstinence.

Liberty cannot live without law, unless the soul is permitted to reason. Liberty and light are more than twin sisters; they are one gracious whole, the outward and the inward, the visible and the invisible powers by which the true soul lives. One of the efforts made everywhere in the New Testament is to lift man up and bring him to recognise this fair liberty, and to learn to do all things for their reasons. This is the education of the soul into the real activity of its spiritual nature.

What a revelation this Epistle must have been to many faithful, earnest, conscientious people in Colosse, who were trying to bend themselves to the new ritualism, to starve themselves, to mortify this troublesome body! What a relief! How it must have cleared away the fantastic clouds brooding over that poor church! What a great, clear light must have come in!

What God wants is that we shall be more fully men and women because we are Christians. We are to take our nature and consecrate it to Him, and find it, for the first time, full of its own proper enjoyments. We are to look upon our bodies as sacred things. Forms and ordinances are to be used as servants, and not as masters, of the soul. Religion must not separate us from the duties of to-day, from the bodies given us for our souls to inhabit, from the friendships and intimate associations of this world.

It is a good deal harder to lead the life of St. Paul than to live the life of the Colossians. It is harder to act in the light and liberty of the Gospel than to get a book of laws and refer to it, or to get a confessor, and go to him, and ask, in every puzzle, what to do. To carry in ourselves the intense love of Jesus Christ, to find in Him the perpetual corrective of our actions, to do duty, not under the lash, but under the impulses of the soul— that is the hardest life, but the most blessed life a man or woman can undertake.

And if we struggle on in this imperfect life, we shall catch increasing glimpses of that coming time when we shall live perfectly in heaven.

TWO EPISTLES.

"Unto Timothy, my own son in the faith; Grace, mercy, and peace, from God our Father and Jesus Christ our Lord."—1 TIM. i. 2.

"For I am now ready to be offered, and the time of my departure is at hand."—2 TIM. iv. 6.

ONE thing, I am very sure, we shall learn from the study of the different Epistles of St. Paul, and that is, that each one has its own distinctive character. There is about each one something which does not belong to the others. The character of the writing, the feelings of the writer, and the audience, are different in each.

We are now to consider two Epistles which are personal, written to an individual, not to a church. However clearly a church may stand forth, it is impossible for it to have a distinct individuality such as belongs to a man. However familiar an audience may become to a speaker, even though it may contain always substantially the same persons, it never can have the distinct personality of the individuals to whom he speaks. And the way in which one speaks to a personal friend in private conversation must always be different from the way in which he addresses a body of his fellow-men, however small or familiar that body may be.

The Epistles to Timothy are not merely personal. They bear the impression of the relation of the writer to the person written to. They are the letters of St. Paul, written when he had come to be called "*Paul the aged,*" to another disciple who had joined him in the early part of his ministry, and had become the most trusted of his friends. More than any other, Timothy's mind was filled with the ideas of which St. Paul's mind was full.

Few relations between men are more interesting than that of a man who has been for years doing a work with some younger man, to whom the work is to be given over to finish or to carry on. That work is to pass through new developments and new circumstances which the man who is passing away may not be able to comprehend. But if there is true generosity in the mind of the older man, he always rejoices that the work is to go on after he has passed away. The older gives to the younger promises and opportunities. All that the older man has done is not going to perish with him. His work projects itself into the future. It is not stopped short by the wall of his own death. The younger man, looking back on the experience of the older teacher, which seems to have lasted longer than it really has lasted, gets some sort of background for his own work. That work is not something which he has started, thought out for himself. The older man gives to the younger a sense of a long-continued past; the younger gives to the older a sense of a long-continued future.

Both these Epistles were written near the end of St. Paul's life. The second is the last that we have of his writing. Several of the Epistles were written during the first imprisonment. After his first trial he was released. He had another period of missionary work, and then a second trial at Rome. In the interval he went back to Asia Minor, and visited the old churches founded years ago. He took Timothy once more, and went with him from church to church. At last, on one of these journeys, he passed over his familiar route from Asia into Europe. He left Timothy at Ephesus to do certain work there. During his journey he writes back to Timothy how to conduct the church. The First Epistle is the counsel of an older minister to the younger.

After this St. Paul was arrested again, and carried once more to Rome. It soon becomes apparent that everything is to be different. He is treated more harshly, and subjected to more restraint. He knows the time is drawing near when he is to lay down his life. From the darkness of that dungeon, where the axe is held over his head, he writes the Second Epistle. It is the most pathetic of all his writings. All the past is with him, and all the future. He is deserted by his friends. He sends this epistle like a cry to his younger friend in Ephesus, begging him to come that the Apostle may see his face once more. We do not know whether Timothy went or not. The voice of St. Paul closes with the last verse of the last chapter of the Second Epistle to Timothy. First Thessalonians is the first of St. Paul's writings, and Second Timothy the last. Read them together.

What are the teachings of St. Paul in these epistles? We shall find it has been good for the Christian Church that they have been kept extant from that early day, and are heard to speak still. But we want to hear behind the word the pathetic tremor of his voice that we may see within them their depth and richness. Then let the impression give us earnestness, and rest with deep power upon our souls.

The First Epistle contains two great instructions. First, *he urges the young Apostle to strive earnestly against corruptions of doctrine which were coming in then.* Secondly, he lays down *certain directions about the way in which the church is to be conducted.*

It must interest us to observe how St. Paul treats *Christian doctrine.* It is not as mere doctrine. It is not like one who loves doctrine for the sake of doctrine. Sometimes doctrine seems to become in the minds of Christian teachers a thing desirable for itself, separate from its end. It is the absence of any such tone as that which makes the early part of St. Paul's First Epistle to

Timothy so valuable. "*We know that the law is good if a man use it lawfully; knowing this, that the law is not made for a righteous man, but for the lawless and disobedient, for the ungodly and for sinners, for unholy and profane, for murderers of fathers and murderers of mothers, for manslayers, for whoremongers, for them that defile themselves with mankind. for menstealers, for liars, for perjured persons, and if there be any other thing that is contrary to sound doctrine.*" "*Sound doctrine*" is not a thing separate from its purpose. It is not spoken from heaven merely for the sake of informing men's minds. Is not this the heresy pervading Christian teaching that Christian teachers have thought of doctrine as something given them that they might exercise their minds upon it, rather than as something which came to them in order that what God supremely loves, a holy life, might be built up? The one great thing which has perverted men's study of the Christian Gospels is that men have dared to forget that the Gospel came to a world of sinners that they might be reclaimed from the paths of sin, and brought to righteousness again. Wonderfully few are the mistakes which men make when they read the Bible for *salvation*. Wonderfully few are the men able to read the Bible rightly when they fasten their eyes on it for *speculation*. The soul which goes to the Bible to get the thing for which it was given gets the thing it goes for. The soul laying hold on the heart of the New Testament finds what was in the heart of God. It is expressed by St. Paul in the phrase: "*the will of God, even your sanctification*". It is certainly easy to find in the New Testament the truth of Jesus Christ.

A man comes to the Bible and says, "Is not this strange and mysterious?" And he points to some marvellous proof he seems to have extorted from the plain text of the New Testament. He is using the Bible for that for which it was not given. He is sure to go wrong, and gather from it some strange doctrine, a fantasy which never was in the simple teaching of the Holy Spirit. Another man goes to the Bible hungering for a better life, desiring to escape from sin; weary of the barren sinfulness of this world, he goes to the Bible for a picture of the kingdom of heaven; goes to the Bible to learn how this world can be made the habitation of the holy God. That man can understand, not perhaps every truth there, for there are truths yet to be developed by certain exigencies of the world; but he will come away full of the learning which he at present needs. The New Testament will become to him a Book of Life.

When St. Paul writes back from Europe to Asia, he bids Timothy teach the disciples that the law is to be used *lawfully*. He tells him and them the same lesson which we need. Let us go to our Bible for our Bible's purpose, inspiration, and a law of life, and the idea of what God would have man to be, and the power to become what it is the purpose of our Father that we should become. This is the teaching of the First Epistle to Timothy.

The fundamental thing which Paul said to Timothy was that he should send the Ephesians to the Bible for the Bible's purpose. Always, spirituality is to go back to purity. The idea that man is to be wise with the wisdom of God is to refresh itself with the idea that man is to be good with the holiness of God.

St. Paul goes on to give a great number of directions about the details of church management. Now, these injunctions are not necessarily laws of the Christian church to-day. If we find some phrases which seem to contradict what are the evident necessities of the church in this our time, I see no reason to suppose that we are to take these injunctions as having perpetual power over the Christian church. I think nothing would have surprised St. Paul, while writing to the Ephesians, more than to be told that centuries and centuries afterward men would go into these instructions which he gave to Timothy for the guidance of the Ephesians of that day and make them a law for us, in this distant day, in lands he never dreamed of, in circumstances of which he had no idea. What is the use of this Book? What are we to learn from its teachings here?

It is the everlasting picture of the fact that the church must be organised all the while with clear distinct statutes; and yet that it must be kept alive and filled with the spirit of a deep sense of what the purpose of the church is. There are two great dangers. There is, first, the danger that a church may be full of the idea of a spiritual purpose and abjure the idea of institutions. And the other danger is opposite to that; the danger of thinking that the church exists in her institutions. Such a writing as this meets both dangers. Men cannot say it makes no difference how they behave, that the church has no statutes and ordinances and institutions, when they see how carefully the great Apostle, in the very beginning, laid down the way in which the church was to be conducted. It is the everlasting protest that the church must have these laws. Yet it throbs with the certainty of the consciousness of the great purpose of the church's life. It is filled with a great sense of the value of the Christian soul, for which alone Christian institutions have any right to exist. He who reads in the spirit in which St. Paul wrote will come away saying: " Certainly the church must have organisations, charities, ministries, appointed places, different disciples. If such things were necessary in those early and spontaneous days, they are no less necessary now. But always they are to be kept healthy and in due proportion of importance by the perpetual certainty, living through the whole church that they exist for, and therefore obedient to the necessities of the soul for which the church exists." St. Paul dealt with institutions exactly as he dealt with doctrines. Institutions, like doctrines, exist for the purpose of creating and sustaining the life of God in the soul.

As the necessities of the soul change, Christian institutions must be continually modified, and adapt themselves to the new necessities of the souls that are to use them. He who goes to these Epistles to learn what they really teach, carries away a perfect content that the church should be organised, and a satisfaction with things that often seem petty and minute. It keeps them always dignified to be filled with the great purpose of the culture of the soul. The one great thing for which God sends all His revelations to mankind, for which the Bible was written, for which the Incarnation came, is that man might be made holy with the holiness of God. This great epistle sets for ever Christian doctrines and institutions in their proper light; honouring both but for the purpose which they subserve; honouring them, but never idolising them. That purpose is "*holiness, without which no man shall see the Lord*" here or hereafter.

We want to let our thoughts reach into St. Paul's dungeon, see him chained to a Roman soldier who hated him, looking every moment that the dungeon door should open and a messenger call him to a cruel judgment and a cruel death. We want to feel the longing of the great soul for the great future that lay before him, while he yet rejoices in human sympathy; so that, though he was longing for the things of heaven, he could not be separated from the friends of this earth; crying out for kindred, even while looking for the crown of glory to be given him. It was a noble thing for him to keep his interest in his work to the very end. It is so natural for men who think they are going to die to lose all interest in life. This shows how narrow and selfish their life has been.

You go to some friend whose life has been very busy about some work which has interested him immensely. You tell him, so as to bring conviction, that he will die to-morrow morning. And you see, instantly, every shadow of interest in the things he has been doing thirty or forty years gone. His soul sinks down in despondency, or else is fixed wholly beyond the grave. Would not that be an awful revelation of the way in which he has been living? It is a shame if he does not believe in his work, hope for it, feel the deepest interest in it, when he knows that his hands will soon be compelled to drop it.

A little while ago we saw the great affairs of politics handed over from one party to another. The thing that made it so grand was the continuance of interest. They who laid down the work, if they had been really identified with it, if they really cared for it, looked forward with deep curiosity, with earnest anxiety, to see what would become of the country when the new administration had taken up the work. It was not simply an administration, or a national life, that had rested upon St. Paul, but Christianity. And he was hoping to the very end, and thinking of this Christianity. In his last words he had been telling his disciples how to carry on the work he had been doing. It reminds us of John the Baptist giving his work to Jesus and saying, "*He must increase, but I must decrease*". We can see at once the secret of such depth and richness as that. The man cared for the work itself, in its own intrinsic character, and not simply his own identification with it. Or, if any of us are identified with any good and great work, let us be sure that we are unselfishly identified with it, that we really care for the things themselves! And if the message should come that we are to lay down our work, let us forget what is going to happen to us. It is the noblest death a man can die. When the soldier is stricken down, the question leaps from his heart to his lips how the battle fares. Let him hear of victory, that all is going well, before he breathes his last, and the noble soldier-soul is content. Read through the second Epistle of Timothy, and you will feel the noble spirit of a man who cares for the things of Christ outside of their identification with himself. How ready he is to give up his own life, and to forget the giving up of his own life, in order that, when he is gone, the work of Christ may live and grow!

Then comes the last great chapter, full of personal anticipation. He is always going back and forward in his writings, as one might when writing to his dearest friend in a desultory fashion; sometimes dwelling upon things belonging to Timothy and the church, sometimes upon things belonging to himself. In the epistles to the Thessalonians, the first of all his writings, St. Paul seems to picture the coming of the last days and the immediate return, or the speedy return, of Christ to this world. The kingdom of heaven was to be established here. That was near the beginning of his ministry. He has ripened since then. It is shown in the broadness and simplicity of his later writing. He no longer lays down special doctrines with regard to the last things—telling just how the heavens are to open and Christ is to appear; who is to be raised first; how all things are to be arranged—as in his first Epistle. It is not that his thought of them has changed, but he speaks of them differently now. Everything has become more spiritual. Whether the crown of glory is to be given him in the world beyond the skies or in this old familiar world, that question has all gone out of the Apostle's thought. There is great simplicity in his conception of the future life, of the way in which Christ will bring forward the things belonging to Him from this dispensation to the other. We are taken up with minute definitions and details ; we are almost ready to fight with any one who thinks Christ will come in a different way from our way. By-and-by, if we are really ripening into the Spirit of Christ, we shall be satisfied with the one great truth that Christ will bring together our soul and His soul, and that we must always belong to Him. We shall cease to think, almost cease to care, how this is to be accomplished.

Often this growth comes as a revelation by the death of our dearest beloved. We have speculated this way and that way—of the first and second coming, of the millennial reign, of the first and final resurrection. Some day our dearest friend lies dying, and at last we see him die. And our soul leaps to the one certainty, fastens itself upon the indisputable truth, that the soul belongs to God, and that, if we can live with God in the few years in which we are left behind, we shall not be spiritually separated when the time comes for us to follow the one who has gone before. We shall be *in God*. *In God*, somewhere our soul will find that soul which is in God also.

Do not be afraid when the things that you used to feel made the substance of faith now seem to be but its fringes. It is a certain truth that in Christ is your redemption, and that to be with

Him will be everlasting life, wherever in the universe the soul may dwell. When we stand strong in this assurance, our little notions may drop away, and we shall be secure in the great certainties of God, and the soul, and everlasting life.

The last recorded teachings of St. Paul may be summed up in these four things:—1. All doctrine exists only with reference to the increasing holiness of man. 2. The institutions of the Christian church are always precious; the church must have them; but only for the purposes of the spiritual life; and they are always to be flexible, changing with the changes of the spiritual life which they are intended to promote and sustain. 3. A man who is identified with a work, in a deep spiritual sense, when he is called upon to give it up to another, will keep his interest in the work to the very end. Let me know that I am to die to-morrow morning, and I want to have such an interest in the church, the country, the world, in everything I care for now, as I have never begun to have in my life. I want to see if there is any last thing I can do. 4. The certainty that Christian truth is simple. God's love, Christ's redemption, the Holy Spirit's perpetual presence, the certain happiness of the soul that trusts in Jesus Christ—we want to have hearts in which all these great simple things shall be held as certainties.

EXPOSITION OF THE NINETEENTH PSALM.

"*The heavens declare the glory of God,*" *etc.*—PSALM xix.

ONE reason for the dislike which is often felt for religious doctrine is, that it has been made to occupy a place for which it is neither intended nor fitted. If you take a man and put him in a place that is unfitted for him, you degrade him, not only for that office but for every other office. It has been a great mistake to take doctrine, which is simply the teaching of truth in its true shape, and try to make it fill the place of the whole of Christian life. Doctrine cannot bring the entrance into Christian character itself. Beyond the learning of the richest truth must come life—the entrance of the Divine Spirit to make life in my soul. Because it has been given a place it cannot fill, doctrine has been depreciated again and again in that great system in which it must always lie as a corner-stone.

Another and more superficial reason why many of us tend to depreciate doctrine is, that it seems to be somewhat dry. There is exultation in an appeal to the feelings. We are disposed to listen more willingly to one who says, "Come into this light, and let this glory strike you," than to one who says, " Study if this be not the true teaching which your nature needs ". But we here see that it is possible to take the beautiful truth of God's teaching, and turn it into one of the most glorious of all the Psalms of David. No Psalm sings itself fuller of the glory of the sunrise that comes to the human heart than this Nineteenth Psalm. Behold, with what majesty and beauty truth can be clothed! We have here the whole education of the human heart. If the story of the building of the heavens and the earth be glorious, how much more glorious the story of the building of the soul!

The Psalm begins with a description of the heavens of nature ; but the description of nature is the key-note to the description of mankind. *" The heavens declare the glory of God."* Man comes to nature for such various things. He comes, in the first place, to pluck the fruits that are growing there to support life. Then he comes to feel the mysterious connection between human nature and all that other nature by which he is surrounded. He rests himself with the perpetual freshness of the universe. He lives with nature, as a brother with a sister, continually linking his life to hers. Then there is another conception ; a very deep conception of the great truth that this world is God's world. Wondrous is the way in which man may learn, more and more, the deepest things out of this nature by which he is surrounded! No words could be so fitly inscribed above the temples of our modern science as these opening words of this Nineteenth Psalm.

How strange it is that we should sometimes fear that, the more man knows about this outer world, the more he will go away from God! Why should Christians desire to shut their eyes and their brothers' eyes, as if the study of nature would draw them away from the God of nature? Everything which the scientific mind discovers of the richness of the natural world leads to that greater, stronger love of God, which will come by-and-by. The real faithlessness is that lack of faith which makes men fear that the knowledge of this world, which God has made, shall not tend, at last, to make men know more of their Heavenly Father, and understand more perfectly His ways. This great Psalm of David will come back at last and tell us of the end, as it has told us of the beginning, of man's study of the natural world.

All nature is teeming with truth. Man goes forth into nature, looks everywhere and finds truth, and behind every truth he finds *the* Truth, which is God.

The whole idea of the latter part of this Psalm is, God, found by man in nature, impresses man with a sense of perfectness of the Divine precepts. See how positive these are. We are apt to talk about God's laws as if they were intended to hold us away from something which ought not to be committed. There is not a word in this wonderful Nineteenth Psalm of duty simply as restraint. Duty is always represented here as something which the soul is permitted to do. "*The law of the Lord is perfect, converting the soul.*" "*The testimony of the Lord is sure, making wise the simple.*" And so on. The highest dealings of God with men are the perpetual indulgences of the human life.

"*The law of the Lord is perfect, converting the soul.*" Afterwards he speaks of the "*commandments*". Law means not simply injunctions, but that great sense of duty which belongs to any knowledge of God on the part of the human soul. God does not give me this and that law. He gives me His law—that is, He gives me Himself as law. As I try to go wrong, there is that duty, bringing the life of God behind me, telling me I must not go that way; I must turn and go this way. The nature of God, teeming with beautiful relations to the nature of man, is always converting the human soul, turning it from that way in which it ought not to go, and turning it into that way in which it ought to go. God is not simply a perpetual Ruler, bringing one large compulsion on me, making right right and wrong wrong for me.

"*The testimony of the Lord is sure, making wise the simple.*" Testimonies are actual statements by the God of truth. The term includes everything that God has made known to man, from God's own existence on through the whole range of Revelation

—His Creatorship, the history of this world, everything known to mankind which man could not have known except by Revelation—and there is nothing which mankind could have known if God had not in some way revealed it.

The word "*simple*" declares of man that he has not much wisdom, does not understand a great deal. But it is not a contemptuous word. It applies to the child-soul in its relations to the father's soul. The child is simple in virtue of his relation to the father. To the simple soul comes testimonies of Almighty God, revelations of wondrous truth. And just because the simple soul receives them as from God, the child is able to take instructions sent down by the great, wise Father.

"*The statutes of the Lord are right, rejoicing the heart.*" The statutes of the Lord are something different from commandments. Commandments I suppose to be, in a more special way, things which belong to temporal conduct. Statutes are more immediate, arbitrary regulations, not having root in the fundamental relation of things. They have their reason in the perception of God as to what will be to the advantage of the human soul. They rejoice the heart. They give a sense of the character of Him who instituted them. They are known to be right from their perceived value and usefulness. As the soul again and again comes to the Lord's Supper, it learns to love that Lord's

Supper, partly because it is the Lord's injunction, partly from tasting how good and sweet it is.

Then comes the large word "*commandment*". Commandments are declarations which belong to all life. Statutes, under the Christian scheme, represent sacraments; commandments, the whole of the duties appearing in all our individual life, in the home, in the office, everywhere growing out of our relations to one another.

"*The commandment of the Lord is pure, enlightening the eyes.*" It is a thing through which the light comes. Shut man out from duty, take away all obligation from the soul, and he sinks into torpidity and darkness. Every new commandment gives to man another duty, becomes a new light. Vivacity, activity, perspicacity, come out from the commandments which a man is engaged in obeying.

"*The fear of the Lord is clean, enduring for ever.*" The fear of the Lord lies behind commandments and statutes. The fundamental relationships to God make us do duty, make us walk in the way of the statutes. And the knowledge of these relations is purifying. It maketh clean the soul. Have we not found in our lives obscurity and confusion brought into the notion of the fear of God? But it need not be so. The fear of God is the understanding of something we ought to do, because He who is greater than we has given it to us to do. How the clouds would pass off and the coldness be taken away, if we could perceive that to fear God is to get hold of something not temporary, not mixed with any corruption, something that is clean and enduring for ever!

"*The judgments of the Lord are true and righteous altogether.*" Judgments are distinct from all voices speaking to man out of the skies. Judgments are outward treatments. God comes to the soul, not merely in the commandments which He speaks, not merely in the truths and revelations of His book; but He is continually teaching us in all the treatment of our lives. The father teaches his child, not merely with his lips or from a book, but by his judgments, by the way in which his own life is continually correcting and suggesting life to the child. The imperfections of the father's teaching come from his liability to mistake. But "*the judgments of the Lord are true and righteous altogether*".

David is not able to compose one single verse which shall be adequate to describe the commandments of God. So he rolls back the curtain from his own experience. He remembers how God has touched his life through all the years in which God and he lived together. So his great words roll on in a lengthened chorus. He cannot restrain himself with simple definition. "*More to be desired than gold, yea, than much fine gold, sweeter also than honey and the honey-comb.*" "*In keeping of them there is great reward.*" God's life has touched his life, and he has felt the blissfulness of being touched by it.

These six great touches of God's hand David talks about. How serious, how strong, are his words! How different from the Twenty-fourth Psalm! That is like the blast of a trumpet, hardly articulate. Here this great master stands before the human race and tells it of God.

The sacredness of our human life is in this: that it should be touched by the hand of God. We must go forth saying, "What a wondrous thing to live! That I, in my insignificant life, should be so cared for by God; that with His touches He is ever trying to shape my life and make it plastic in the form He would have it be!" What an ambition will come into the heart and soul of men when they have entered into the spirit of this great Psalm! Men will then say, "If God so cares for my life, I will care for it too. I will care to go on through that journey to that end."

We may see now where doctrine takes its place in our lives. That which has seemed dry and dusty becomes all alive with inspiration and with fire. The soul is sent on to glory to fulfil that design for which God cares so much. It is a great deal to know that God cares to tell us truth. It is a great deal when the father tells the child that this is so or that is so. It is a great deal more when the father so values his child that he thinks it worth while to instruct him in the deepest reasons.

If we go on, year after year, through life, conscious each year that God is teaching us, then more valuable than any special lessons will be the touches that He lays upon our lives; that rich, deep, beautiful sense that God does care what becomes of us; that there is something about every one of us so precious that God thinks it worth while to lavish upon us His law, and testimonies, and statutes, and commandments, His fear and His judgments.

EXPOSITION OF THE TWENTY-THIRD PSALM.

WE ask ourselves, as we read this psalm, and see how it can be taken up by the Christian consciousness, Is there anything in the religious life outside of Christianity that shows such trust in God? The answer we give, and are glad to give, is that in its degree only is the psalm peculiar to Christianity. No soul outside of redemption, represented in its immaturity by Judaism and in its maturity by Christianity, has such entire trust in God as is represented here. The difference would almost always be that the soul, in very few of the psalms of other religions, keeps its own absolute personality and distinctness. There are psalms of the pantheistic religions in which the soul seems to lose itself in the great current of the Divine Being, and become but one drop in the ocean of universal existence. They have the idea of rest and repose and freedom from disturbance and trouble. But in this psalm there is something different. There is, indeed, the individual consciousness of love resting on the soul, that still has its own right to live and to know its past.

Every religion bears its testimony to us of God dwelling in human nature. I do not know of a religious yearning of mankind in any part of his spiritual history which has not sought to see beyond the clouds the peace of God resting on the human soul. That is the great mission of religion in the human soul. The Christian religion, above all, means rest and peace and final reconciliation to God as the great outcome of it all. That is the reason Christianity is able to bear so much of distress, and come triumphantly through it; because it continually recognises peace beyond as the condition of the human soul.

There are times in our experience when we are inclined to overstate the necessity for turmoil in the soul. There are times when we ought to say, "It will not do for the soul to rest in peace; *woe unto them that are at ease in Zion*". The soul at times needs to be disturbed and broken-hearted; but always in anticipation and preparation for the calm that lies beyond. The ultimate condition of the human soul is repose, such as fills the sweet, rich verses of this psalm of David.

It is the record of an experience marked all over with the vicissitudes of life. A man simply tossed into existence, and lighting on the back of some great, quiet, and restful condition, and who had been there always, could not have written this psalm. Think how different a psalm of repose he would have written! It is a man who has been through great experiences who thus lifts up his voice and sings to God in absolute trust in the Divine goodness and strength. These words come not only as brother words to other souls dwelling in the same peace, but to souls struggling as he had struggled. David stands forth and lifts up his voice, and says, "Struggle on, O my brethren, struggle for the deeper and sweeter peace in God to which you will attain".

We are apt to think about the Old Testament as if it were hard and rigid and rugged and severe and stern. Some people say, "I like the New Testament very much, but I do not care to read the Old Testament"; but right in the midst of the Old Testament shines the Twenty-third Psalm, as if it were put there in order that men might never dare to call that book harsh and hard and severe and stern. This psalm is an outpouring of the soul to God, never matched in all the riches of the Christian day. It is the utterance of a soul absolutely unshaken and perfectly serene. There are times when everything in God's dealings with us seems to be stern and hard and bitter; then, just as we are ready to cast ourselves away in despair, and feel toward God as toward a ruler whom we can simply fear but never love, there comes some manifestation of God that sets our soul to singing. The hardest and severest passages in the Old Testament find relief if we let the light shine on them from the Twenty-third Psalm.

In the New Testament many of the expressions of deepest faith have their origin in this psalm. "*The Lord is my shepherd, I shall not want.*" See how one of the words which afterwards became the inheritance of the race first came to be used. Many words have passed into common use and are now used without any feeling of their sacred origin in the local circumstances out of which the Bible was first written. This is the case with the word "*shepherd*". David, the shepherd boy, had been back and forth over the fields of Judea, and, in the care of those dependent on him, had learned to feel the care of the heavenly Father. It is a beautiful thing when the soul, from its own relationship toward dependent ones, comes to recognise the care of God. Taking up the lamb in his arms, David thought: "So my heavenly Father will carry me through all the days of my life". Our Saviour said: "*I am the good shepherd*". He took the figure from the Old Testament, and when His disciples came to do the work He had done, the title "shepherd," or "pastor," became universal in Christian history. The pastors of the flock are they who try, in their weakness and inability, to do that which Christ did perfectly. David could find no word to describe more fully to his own mind the richness of the care that God had for his life, the absolute dependence of his life upon God's love, than that taken from his own daily occupation.

"*I shall not want.*" There are two ways of not lacking a thing in this world. He lacks nothing who has everything. If one could take the stars from the sky, and the rivers from their beds, he might say, "I lack nothing". To get everything possible for the soul to want is one way of saying, "I want nothing". The better way is for a man to look up and bring his desires down to that which God sees fit to give him. This applies emphatically to things of faith. If I knew all the mysteries of God, I might say, "I lack no knowledge of God". But if, knowing only what God has told me, I let all the gaps in my knowledge go because He has not chosen to fill them, in a richer sense I may say, "I lack no knowledge of God". May that be our portion! May we come to contentment long, long before we have possessed everything! Since we know that God has given us everything it is good for us to have, may we be content!

"*He maketh me to lie down in green pastures; He leadeth me beside the still waters.*" There are two ways by which we may come to green pastures and still waters. God had led David into sweet and beautiful circumstances, where it was easy for him to walk. But his words must have meant something deeper than that. A place is not simply a thing of the outward life. It is a thing of the inward life. The soul in the midst of mountains and tempests and torrents, if it keep its relations to God, may still be among the still waters and the green pastures. It is something it carries within itself. To go with calm soul, because it calmly trusts in God, in the midst of tempests and tumults, and say, " I am at peace and rest "—that is the triumph of the Christian state. First of all comes a peaceful condition within the soul. By-and-by comes the kingdom of heaven, with all its scenery. But first there must be a kingdom of heaven within you, that finds its peace, no matter what storms are raging around.

" *He leadeth me in the paths of righteousness for His name's sake.*" The poor soul is not able to think of itself as precious enough to deserve all the care of God. It loves to think that God is taking care of him for His own sake because it is precious to Himself; as the child, to reassure himself of the father's care, says, " My father values me as part of his own existence, therefore he will take care of me ". Many a time the soul has to flee from the sense of its own little value to the thought that God values it because it is dear and precious to Himself.

"*Yea, though I walk through the valley of the shadow of death, I will fear no evil, for Thou art with me: Thy rod and Thy staff they comfort me.*" With what preciousness these words clothe themselves when spoken by the dying, or by those who are trying to arm themselves better for the death of such as are dear to them! The blackness of darkness in this word death is dreadful and sad; but every soul must walk through it. It seems as if God would be shut out from our sight in the dark valley. David says, "*Thy rod and Thy staff they comfort me*".

The sheep go with the shepherd through the sunlit fields, and in the darkness they walk together, though they cannot see each other. Only by the touches of the rod and the staff upon the sheeps' sides here and there can the shepherd guide them. Does not this perfectly correspond to many of the ways in which God guides us in our darker moments? It seems as if we had lost our clear visions, and we are clouded and disturbed by the anxieties of life; then the Lord guides us by touches of His rod and His staff on this side and on that side, by persuasions and dissuasions, by intimations of His will. Though we have none of the rich joy which comes from seeing His face, He keeps us from wandering too far, until at last the sunshine comes again, and the rod and the staff are laid aside, no more needed, because we see our leader face to face.

"*Thou preparest a table before me in the presence of mine enemies.*" This does not mean separation from our enemies, nor driving them away. God reaches out His hand and says, "Lie down here in the presence of your enemies, and eat in peace at the table which I have spread for you". Not only when we come to where we shall have trodden Satan under foot, but in the midst of the battle, raging behind, before, around us, we are to come to where the Lord spreads our table. He says, " Sit down here and eat, and I will make the enemy wait until, by your eating, you shall be ready to stand up and fight the battle through ". By giving us peaceful moments in the midst of the distress and the struggle of our lives He spreads a table before us in the presence of our enemies.

" *Surely goodness and mercy shall follow me all the days of my life, and I will dwell in the house of the Lord for ever.*" David's temple was more to him than our churches ought to be to us. We live in a larger temple. Ours is a broader conception of God's presence than David could possibly have. We may say to ourselves, " *I will dwell in the house of the Lord,*" certain that in faithfulness to the duties of life, in steadfastness under the pressure of care, every occupation, every house, may be to us *the house of the Lord*. The house of the Lord is this universal world. The rooms of our house are in every possible experience. Our church life should be something between the temple life of David and the rich life foretold in the Revelation, where there is to be no temple.

Could there be a psalm more full of peace than this ? For every sorrow that comes to man it provides absolute consolation. It is written not simply for David, with his experience, but for all the experiences that would come to men.

Let your souls rest in peace on God. Only be sure it is really He on Whom you rest. He is continually caring for your souls, and will not let you rest in absolute torpor. You cannot rest too peacefully, too tenderly, on the love of God, if only it is really God's love.

This psalm is a picture of that wonderful life which we dream of as coming some time, which we are almost impatient to have come at once, in which we shall serve God as we have never been able to serve Him here, and trust in His care with a sense of His love deeper and more complete than we now can know.

EXPOSITION OF THE FIFTY-NINTH PSALM.

IN order to place ourselves in a position to understand these Psalms it is necessary to remember the conditions under which communications are made between God and men. Although God manifests Himself in many ways, any complete revelation to the human race must always be through humanity. And this revelation through humanity is made not merely by words, but by all the means through which man communicates thoughts or emotions to man.

In the parable of the husbandmen we are taught that God sent into the world many different kinds of messengers; and at last He sent His Son. If we turn back to the prophets of the Old Testament, we shall feel in them less personality than in Jesus. We can conceive of the words of Isaiah or Jeremiah being sent abroad into the world without any personal medium. But when Jesus came all was different. If it were possible for Jesus always to live and manifest Himself on earth, we might conceive of His words not being preserved. The person of Jesus Christ would be the great manifestation of God under the New Testament dispensation.

A complete revelation is not in words simply, but in individual life—a manifold dispensation through various activities. Think of the lives that you have known in your existence here. While you remember precious words spoken by those with whom you have come in contact, the words are not the real revelation made to you by your friends. Think of the greatest teacher with whom you have had communication. Suppose you were offered the choice of either of two things : to keep a perfect remembrance of every word, the intrinsic truth to be continually with you; or to retain the force of his personality, to be allowed to keep personal impressions of character and life, while forgetting every word that was ever uttered. Can you doubt for a moment which you would select? However precious the words might be, you would gladly let them all go, that you might keep the impress of character. You look back and remember how he acted, how he bore himself in the different experiences of life. Out of all his activities comes one impression of his character, stamping itself upon your character in a way which would be impossible for any uttered words. All the best manifestations come through characters acting upon our lives.

Greater, always, than the Bible is the Christ of whom the Bible tells us. Let us have the reality of Jesus in our hearts, and we might let Matthew, Mark, Luke and John be forgotten if we could keep the impression of His personality.

Bear this in mind always in reading the Psalms of David. They contain words of great wisdom, words of precious truth. But in the words is not their supreme value. That which gives the Book of Psalms its supreme value, which has made it the book of all centuries, that in it which has impressed so many souls with the power of God, is its revelation of human nature. The strong richness of that great humanity, manifested by one who, starting as a shepherd boy, became the ruler of the Jews has left its impress upon all history. David comes to us through David's Psalms. And the great value of the Psalms is that they let us know David, his character, and the way God treated him. In the Psalms human nature in its relation to God is revealed as it never has been in any other writings in all time.

Now, apply this to the Fifty-ninth Psalm. David here invokes all sorts of evil upon his enemies. The words burn out of a fiery heart. He calls upon God not to spare them. "Slay them not, lest Thy people forget; scatter them by Thy power, and bring them down." He begs God not to grant them the merciful cruelty of death, not to take them from the world, but to torture them in their boastful pride, that their fate may be a perpetual warning.

How harsh! how cruel! Turn back to the Psalm preceding, where David prays against his enemies: "Break their teeth, O God, in their mouth; break out the great teeth of the young lions, O Lord!" There is no doubt about the character of words like these. Try to put them over into the New Testament, into the lips of Him whom David imperfectly represented: think of Jesus standing in the midst of His enemies and saying words like these, and you will feel how terrible they are.

When we read such psalms in public worship or in the private study of the Psalter, what do they mean to us? We want to enter very deeply into the meaning of these words, and know what place they have in this great book we call the Bible.

And this starts one or two questions in regard to the Bible that need to be started in our time. It is said, sometimes, that these Psalms were used in daily worship, perhaps by David himself, as prophecies of what was certain to come upon evildoers; that it is necessary for men to know that no evil can be done which shall not bring mischief upon the evil-doers; that it is not best for men to think they can be good or bad, just as they please, and no evil befall them. It is said that men need to be reminded that no evil can be done without bringing pain somewhere upon those who do it; and that the enemies of God must learn that they are setting themselves against the great order of things, and shall certainly be punished. Comparison is made with that chapter in which Jesus declares the great evils that are coming upon the world, and it is maintained that the same idea belongs to that as to this; that it is not invocation, but prophecy of evil. It is impossible, in the world of God, to be bad and not suffer, to do wickedness and not receive the pain belonging to wickedness.

Another explanation is, that David wrote, not out of his own heart, from a sense of personal wrong—so I think I have heard it stated—but that he denounced the enemies of God as God's enemies, not his own; not because they had wronged David, but because they had wronged David's Master. According to this view, such Psalms are the expression of a great, holy indignation in the soul of a man full of love to God. I am reminded that, if I love God, it is impossible for me to look without indignation upon those who dishonour God, and hurt His children, and interfere with His great purposes; that I cannot but let come, bursting out, strong, hard, true words, like those in Psalms lviii. and lix.

Such, then, are the explanations that are offered of the "denunciatory" Psalms: that they are either anticipations of what is certain to come upon the doers of wickedness, or declarations of what ought to come upon the enemies of God everywhere, and are entirely free from personal feeling.

To all which I simply say : it is perfectly legitimate to associate these two meanings with these Psalms. The two meanings are there. But, as I shall say in a moment, they do not seem to me to be the characteristic or principal meanings.

It is, indeed, impossible to read the words without recognising references to the enemies of God, and declarations that the enemies of God must suffer; without hearing the great and solemn prophecy that not simply great sinners, but we, if we stand in the way of any work of God, must suffer pain. I should like to think that we recognise these two true and simple meanings.

But, as I said before, this is not what David meant by the "denunciatory" Psalms. It is impossible to think that this was the meaning in his mind, or, at all events, that this exhausts the meaning in his mind. The words are too hot for that. They have too deep a sense of personal emotion. They mean wrong against those who had done him wrong. They mean hate toward those who hated him. Seeming to have control of the thunders of the universe, he calls them down upon those who had injured him, for the injustice poured upon his head.

This Psalm was written by David when the messengers of Saul had gone out to seek him. Once and again they had tried to murder this young man. You will find an account of the circumstances in the nineteenth chapter of the First

Book of Samuel. Emissaries of Saul went scouting and prowling in search of David, like evil beasts snarling about in Eastern cities. "They make a noise like a dog, and go round about the city." It is a picture of what may be seen to-day in those Eastern cities, where dogs may be seen running about from house to house seeking something to devour.

David wrote in the spirit of personal rage. He was angry with Saul and those whom Saul sent to kill him. He deemed no punishment too great for them, no vengeance he could call down from heaven too strong.

Shall we blame him for such a spirit as that? Certainly we ought to. These Psalms are not the picture of an ideal man, the story of a perfect life; they are not written down as the unimpeachable utterances of a human soul's devotions. They are the utterances of a great, strong, godly human being, full of sores, imperfections, and corruptions. David's Psalms exhibit his character in his own words, and show what manner of man he was, just as it is shown in the great historic books by the narrative of his life. We are to read these Psalms for our instruction. They give us every side of his life—his failures, as well as successes, his weakness, as well as strength. His great soul comes pouring out, that we may recognise the evil, as well as the good in him.

What are the lessons to be learned by a congregation reading such Psalms in unison or by any one reading them alone? 1. They are the utterances of a profound trust in God. David turns to God in his need for that which he thinks ought to be done in the world. Instead of turning to himself, he turns to God, and lays hold on His hand for some sort of vengeance. 2. They show a deep consciousness of the difference between sin and goodness, and a deep certainty that every evil will be punished. 3. But David is unable to separate God's cause from his own; and so he is ready to denounce God's punishment against his own enemies.

A wholly different idea comes to every man from the pages of the New Testament—the idea of forgiveness and prayer for enemies. Shall we take the words of Jesus and put them on the lips of David? Ascribe to him those great words of Christ: "Father, forgive them, for they know not what they do," and you will feel how strangely they come in. If anything seems to make these words of David right, they would be convicted in a moment by putting them in the midst of the words of Christ. The imperfect life of David and the perfect life of Jesus could not be more absolutely contrasted than by taking the Fifty-ninth Psalm and placing it in close comparison with the words of Jesus upon the cross.

People are continually reading these Psalms in the services of the church and in the study of the

Bible. It is not good that the people should not understand how they really are to be read. The conscience becomes confused and twisted if it tries to think that everything in the Psalms is the true sentiment for Christians to take upon their lips.

This idea is a part of our preposterous way of treating the Bible as if it were one whole book, dropped in some mysterious moment altogether out of heaven. It is a historical book, gradually developing its rich spiritual life. It grows to completion only in Christ. The Bible is not a stream which starts and runs unchanged down to the sea. In its earlier course it partakes of the imperfection of the banks between which it starts. It runs through deep soil, and carries part of the soil with it. It only gradually purifies itself. At length it comes to the place where it is seen as a river running along in perfect purity over its rocky bed. It starts in the midst of all the corruptions of the old Hebrew life, and of the people back of the Hebrew life who came before the Hebrews were a nation. It flows down, gradually purifying itself from its corruption. Abraham leaves his wickedness in the stream, Moses leaves his, David his, Isaiah his. By-and-by it comes to run through a great rock of salvation, where there is nothing but the richness and depth and goodness of the life of Jesus Christ. If we attempt to go back and make everything that Abraham and Moses and David did absolutely right, we shall only make the whole stream seem foul. If the Fifty-ninth Psalm is right, the words on the Cross are not right. But if Christ shows us the way we ought to feel toward our enemies, if His words teach the soul of man what are the consummate utterances of a wronged personal soul, then this Psalm of David is harsh and brutal and revengeful. And so it is.

As we read it we understand how, in the midst of a great spiritual life, of a soul very close to God, which God claims, which God is educating by deep experiences, there may still linger the corruptions of the old fierce nature. And this understanding may make us more hopeful in regard to ourselves, more patient in regard to our brethren.

I may hope that, corrupted as the Divine life in me now may be, it will ultimately come to purity; for I see how, in this great man, corruption existed in the midst of the Divine life which he lived. Some one near me claims to be a Christian, to be living for high purposes. Yet, behold! he is not without the frailties of human life. He comes to the communion table and accepts the invitation: " Ye that do truly and earnestly repent of your sins, and are in love and charity with your neighbours, and intend to lead a new life, following the commandments of God, and walking henceforth in His holy ways, draw near with faith and take this holy sacrament." Shall I deny his spiritual life? Shall I say his profession is all hypocrisy and sham? Not if I will take the character of David, and see how, as shown in the Fifty-ninth Psalm, the remnants of the old carnal life still lingered in this fierce and furious man, while at the same time he was the servant of God.

How this picture comes close home to our personal life! To return to the figure of the stream. We, too, live in a weak condition; the stream of our spiritual life is clouded by muddy passions. And we, too, may look forward to the time when the stream, always gradually being purified, shall at last become absolutely pure and perfect in its entire identification with Christ.

TRUE GREATNESS.

"Thy gentleness hath made me great."—PSALM xviii. 35.

THE eighteenth psalm is a recital of all the goodness which had crowned the life of David. The words of our text teach us that human greatness is the result of God's gentleness. Let us define, if possible, what greatness is. It is what we are all striving after according to our own individual idea; and yet, if we ask, who can tell us what "greatness" is? We have the vaguest notions of it. The boy dreams of it, the man struggles after it, the old grey-head fumbles for it among the ashes of dead hopes.

But true greatness consists in being the best and doing the best that our nature is capable of. It is making the most of ourselves. This definition will bring many within the ranks of the great whom the world knows not as such; and it will cut off many who think themselves great, or are so esteemed among men. One characteristic of true greatness is that there is nothing partial or one-sided about it; it is the full, complete development of all our powers; whereas we, in our false estimate of life, often think that striking and powerful things are truly great.

But look at Nature. Her greatest works are not her most noisy or most terrible ones. The Alpine torrent, the glacier, the gorge give us but one-sided views of their Maker's greatness. It is the silent influences, the secret might of Nature, that are the fullest of power and greatness. The ripening of the grain on a summer's day beneath the full sun—this is instinct with greatness. We pass by, unnoticed, the corn-field and the orchard when we are looking for instances of God's greatness; and yet there is nothing so full of the completeness of His power, the "gentleness that maketh great".

Your child, in a darkened room, sees one ray of sunlight coming through the closed shutters, and exclaims, "How wonderful!" Yet take him out into the full, broad sunlight of noon and he sees no wonder, no greatness there. He plays his little games unmindful of the greatness of the perfect day.

To get an idea of God's gentleness, and how it maketh great, look again at Nature. Her quiet and silent influences are always the mightiest. The crag frowns, the torrent rages, the storm howls. There is something cruel about them all. But in the sunshine and the corn-field we may see the most perfect development of power—nothing one-sided or partial.

Look, too, at the family, the most perfect type of God's government. The child is educated and moulded by the union of the father's and the mother's love. Both together make up the power of gentleness. A child who has lost either father or mother is deprived of something which can never be made up to it by the one who is left. But in God we know both a father's and a mother's love—discipline and tenderness in one. God's gentleness hath made us great.

As always, we must look to Jesus Christ as the fullest, highest expression of the truth of our text. He is the incarnate gentleness of God. In Him we see the omnipotence of gentleness, and the gentleness of omnipotence. The gentle God comes and walks among men, giving light to the blind, healing to the leper, raising the widow's son—doing all the great and gentle works of God.

As of old, in the days of Elijah, so it is now in our own lives and their lessons. The " great and strong wind " may rend the mountains and " break in pieces the rocks before the Lord " ; but the Lord is not in the wind ; and after the wind, an earthquake ; but the Lord is not in the earthquake ; and after the earthquake, a fire ; but the Lord is not in the fire ; and after the fire, " a still small voice ".

MAKING ALL THINGS NEW.

We hear men talk of God a century ago, and it is as if they talked of an artificer, a carpenter, a builder, who stood somewhere out of His world, and then, having made it, and sent it forth as if it were a ship upon the ocean, only let it come back to Him as it needed repairs. If there is a great thought that has come to men's minds, it is that God is not outside of His world, but that He is inside it. He is perpetually leading it on from instant to instant, so that we are sometimes almost inclined to lose it in Him and Him in it. Thus we feel that the whole conception of God and His relation to the world to-day shows the rich meaning of those words that have come down to us through the ages, "Behold I, this living power, this living principle, I make all things new".

And it seems to me that one of the ways in which this word of God is perpetually being verified, and is perpetually becoming a blessed consciousness to us, is in the way that we are constantly assured that the newness of the world must be in the newness of its human creatures. It is not that the world changes; it is that man changes.

The world might not be the same; but, if men were the same, it would still be a monotony. All things must be forever new to every man. Think how they are new to every man who comes into the world. The world deals out its systems of philosophy, it accumulates its rich store of experience; and then every new child that is born into the world has to begin again, as if he were the first one. Sorrow, joy, friendship, enmity, all these experiences of men's souls, we learn about when we are children. We cannot *know* them till they come to us. They are born anew to every new man. Columbus sails across the ocean and finds America; and it seems as if he had found it for all voyagers since. Yet every new ship and every new voyager discover it again. So the age is born anew for every soul that enters it. Who can tell what the world is for any one of his brethren? I often think that I would like to be one of my fellow-creatures, it matters not who, for ten minutes, that I might know what it is for that man. There is something awful in the thought that a man goes through these threescore years and ten, and is always simply himself; that he does not know how the sunshine appears, how the world seems, how the skies bend over the head of any one but himself. We get some glimpses of how the world reports itself to others. What are those miracles of Jesus, over which the world disputes, except the recognition by the world of its

Master who speaks to it? This world is so much more to Him than it was to His ancestors who knew so little of its secret, who had entered so little into its largest confidence, showing more complete obedience to the Master of its life when He stands in its midst. If Christ be a manifestation of God, miracle is the very first condition of His life. I look for it the very moment that I know His nature. The world turns its new side, its deeper being, out to Him, as it turns a new side to every man who has looked into it, and claimed the mastery over the world in which God has set him as its lord.

So, if the world is made new with every creature, what is the expectation for the future? Not only that each man is going to be grander and stronger, but that humanity is to be stronger. The whole race moves forward. Not only occasionally, but steadily and solemnly, the whole great life of man moves on. Who can tell what this obedient earth, so richly yielding her resources, so observant of the power and life of man, is going to be to man in the years to come? A new heaven and a new earth must come to claim it. The only way for us to make a new world is to be forever new men. The only way for us to take upon our lips a new song, to count God's mercies new every morning, is to be perpetually new men, to find our lives new with every rising of the sun. Oh, the great depth of that word of the

Master, who said to His disciple, "Thou must be born again"! To Nicodemus, who asked for new laws and new arrangements, the Master said, "You must be a new man".

Do you ever dread the tedium of life? Does it ever seem to you that, bright as life is at its entrance, it must by and by become monotonous? As if the ever rising and setting of the sun, the ever going on of the seasons, the everlasting repetition of those laws and routines which the social and political life of man has beaten out, must become wearisome and dead with their constant reiteration? What is the prospect, unless there is every new day a deeper life for every child of God, a deeper conception of his Father's nature, his Father's influence, and his Father's love? And the great truth is that He who makes men new with every beginning day makes the world new with every beginning day.

Let us pray for a new birth, not as one experience, but as the perpetual experience of our lives; for such nearness to our God that every day He shall give us something more of Himself, be something more to us, so that, being ourselves forever new, the whole world may forever have richness and abundance and variety and beauty and interest and joy and education to give us, so long as we live.

THE GREAT DEEDS OF CHRIST.

IF we can enter into the company of Christ, and live there, then our unknown possibilities shall open to us, and in the light of those unknown possibilities we shall be able to despise and to escape from the baser things that cling to us. Do you remember how Christ went snapping this chain and that chain among the sons of men whom His life touched? Nicodemus came to Him, and the creed-bound Pharisee became the faith-clad man. Christ came to the poor Magdalene, and, in her sin, He touched her, and she lifted herself up and was free, not only from her sin, but from the tyranny of her dark remorse, and entered into His service, and by-and-by was with Him at His crucifixion. He came to twelve plain men, and touched their lives, and each and every one of those men became that which any one of us would give His life if he might become—one of the apostles of the new redemption, one of the saviours of the world.

Has there been nothing since? Has it limited itself to the story told in those few pages? Has it not gone down through history? What shall you make of the heroisms and the martyrdoms, and of the men who have counted not their lives dear to them, that they might bear witness to the truth? What of the men who have languished in prisons and burned at stakes that Christ might do some of His work in them? In the old days they used to cry out, when they saw the Christian, "There is the coming martyr!" When the Christian looked into the sky he always saw his cross there, drawing nearer and nearer to him, sure that he should hang on it. *"Christiani ad leones!"*— "The Christians to the lions!"—used to be the cry. Is it all gone? Has heroism died out of the world? Has it passed away, this capacity in men for giving themselves to noble ends? Are there no lions for the Christian still? Ah! we think ourselves satisfied if the young Christian not merely does not go to the lions, but if we can save him from going to the dogs. Nay, surely there is in the human soul—we in this generation have seen it—a power of self-sacrifice which the emergency calls forth. I never shall remember the days of twenty-five years ago, and not know that every man I look in the face is bigger and greater than he seems to be. And when, across the self-sacrifice of those great days, which some of us remember, I see far off the greater sacrifices of those who gave themselves for the salvation of the world, and were like Jesus Christ, I am sure of this, that there are mysterious powers and depths of sacrifice in every man, ready to open when they shall be called for, only to know that they are called for every day, only to know that, not in any great disturbance that shakes the world, but in the perpetual needs, in the continual miseries, in the abundant sins of life, there is the demand for that which is in you; and you must believe it yourself, like Christ, and respond to the demands of your life, which is very often a great deal harder than the lives that men lived when the stakes were burning. The more I live the more becomes to me wonderful and infinite the mystery of human life. To be a human creature is a wonderful thing. The poorest little urchin upon the street whom you may see when you go out has in him such a mystery. It is such a wonderful thing that he should be what he is, it seems as if the most wonderful mystery were hardly higher—that Luther, Shakespeare, Plato are hardly more wonderful than that poor urchin, who carries in mind and soul and body the wonderful tokens that he is the child of God. To respect in him and to respect in yourself that sonship of God, in the pattern and with the leadership of Jesus Christ—that is the total impulse of religion, that is the liberation of the human soul.

Ah! my friends, it must be a personal following of a personal leader. A creed can never make me believe how wonderful man is, how wonderful I am. It may tell it to me, and the words bound back again from my intelligence on which they strike. A rite or ceremony can never, in itself, force it any further than my fingers and my mouth. But the Master, the personal manifestation of it, the Christ, who is to-day that which He has been in all the ages, He who walks so humble and so strong, so free, because of His absorption, devotion, and consecration to His Father—He brings it to me. And if you will let Him walk with you in streets, and sit with you in your offices, and be with you to your homes, and teach you in your churches, and abide with you as the Living Presence in your hearts, you, too, shall know what freedom is, and, while you do your duties, be above your duties; and, while you live your life, still walk, already walk, in heaven; and while you own yourselves the sons of men, know that you are sons of God.

There are men in this house now, who, if they went out with such a spirit as this, might be small Christs to the men whom they meet. There are men who, if they went forth to every duty, yet knowing the life that is above these daily duties and living in it, might be revelations wherever they went. Their office-boys would feel the difference if they saw them, not slaves to, but masters of their business. Their ordinary companions, as they meet them in the place of traffic, would know the difference if they saw them superior to the thing they did, and therefore doing it all the more nobly, all the more conscientiously, because they did it loftily, in the sight of God. May we so follow Jesus Christ and share in His enfranchisement, may we so enter into this life of liberty which sets us free from all slavery, that already the chains may drop from our hands, that we sometimes foolishly think will drop when the time of dying comes—as if there were some magic in that little thing of dying! Let them drop now, in our lives, and let us now go forth into the glorious liberty of the children of God, into the freedom wherewith the free Christ makes all the obedient children of His Father free.

www.ingramcontent.com/pod-product-compliance
Lightning Source LLC
Chambersburg PA
CBHW030016240426
43672CB00007B/972